Complex PTSD Trauma and Recovery

A STEP BY STEP GUIDE TO SURVIVE FROM PTSD. LEARN TO MANAGE NEGATIVE EMOTIONS, OVERCOME TRAUMA, AND BECOME WHOLE

Bethany Key

Copyright 2020 - All rights reserved.

The content contained within this book may not be reproduced, duplicated or transmitted without direct written permission from the author or the publisher.

Under no circumstances will any blame or legal responsibility be held against the publisher, or author, for any damages, reparation, or monetary loss due to the information contained within this book. Either directly or indirectly.

Legal Notice:

This book is copyright protected. This book is only for personal use. You cannot amend, distribute, sell, use, quote or paraphrase any part, or the content within this book, without the consent of the author or publisher.

Disclaimer Notice:

Please note the information contained within this document is for educational and entertainment purposes only. All effort has been executed to present accurate, up to date, and reliable, complete information. No warranties of any kind are declared or implied. Readers acknowledge that the author is not engaging in the rendering of legal, financial, medical or professional advice. The content within this book has been derived from various sources. Please consult a licensed professional before attempting any techniques outlined in this book.

By reading this document, the reader agrees that under no circumstances is the author responsible for any losses, direct or indirect, which are incurred as a result of the use of information contained within this document, including, but not limited to, - errors, omissions, or inaccuracies.

TABLE OF CONTENTS

INTRODUCTION   7

CHAPTER 1
Understanding PTSD   11

CHAPTER 2
Symptoms of CPTSD   19

CHAPTER 3
PTSD Symptoms Differential Diagnosis   29

CHAPTER 4
Strategies to Recovery   39

CHAPTER 5
Dialectal Behavior Therapy   49

CHAPTER 6
PTSD and Relaxation   59

CHAPTER 7
What Is Psychotherapy?   69

CHAPTER 8
What Is Talk Cure Therapy?   75

CHAPTER 9
What Is Cognitive Behavioral Therapy?   79

CHAPTER 10
What Is Cognitive Processing Therapy?   89

CHAPTER 11
Somatic or "Right-Brain" Psychotherapy   97

CHAPTER 12
What Is EMDR?   103

TABLE OF CONTENTS

CHAPTER 13
Trauma and PSTD—PTSD Treatment
with Hypnotherapy — **115**

CHAPTER 14
Can Medication Help? — **127**

CHAPTER 15
PSTD Methods — **137**

CHAPTER 16
About PTSD & Triggers — **145**

CHAPTER 17
Recovery and Daily Home life Demands — **155**

CHAPTER 18
To Family and Friends — **163**

CHAPTER 19
Curing PTSD with EFT, Meditation,
and Energy — **169**

CHAPTER 20
Trauma Treatment and Mental Health — **177**

CONCLUSION — **181**

INTRODUCTION

Most who are troubled with post-traumatic stress, heal naturally. A few need support. If you suffer from post-traumatic stress disorder (PTSD), I applaud you for looking at this self-help workbook. It can transform your life from living with PTSD to living in an overall peaceful way. In the book, I will describe what PTSD is, show you how to identify whether you have such a problem, and then explain how to get rid of it. The term PTSD is often used, but many times, it is misunderstood. If, for several months or years, a person suffers trying to keep away from remembering what traumatized them, is jumpy and emotionally unavailable, then PTSD is a label to describe the symptoms that person is suffering from. Eliminating PTSD completely is what this book is about, rather than only managing its symptoms. According to robust research that has been repeated for over twenty-five years internationally, the best way of getting rid of PTSD completely is known as 'prolonged exposure therapy.' Before starting the prolonged exposure, it is important to have specific skills in place, such as abilities to relax, think of positive affirmations, and behave in a healthy way. These, too, you can find out how to do, in a step-by-step way, as you read on. For self-treatment, all you need to do is follow the step-by-step guidance in the worksheets so that you can free yourself from PTSD. As you read on, you share my knowledge and understanding of how to release yourself from it, relax, and be more content. Being gripped by anxiety while experiencing contentment is impossible, just as it is not possible to be stressed and feeling anxious while relaxing.

Although treating PTSD can be very complex, I have created this workbook in a way that you can follow, one simple worksheet at a time. There is a theory that many believe: when we are traumatized, we shut down. But when faced with individuals who have been through trauma, this is not the case in front of our eyes because individuals continue bravely on, using their own coping methods; sometimes these strategies are unhealthy. The drug-free psychological techniques I offer you have been used a great many times successfully. As a university senior lecturer, I taught trainee counseling psychologists the method you are about to learn. They used it at their clinical placements with great results for their clients who suffered from PTSD. On account of such successful outcomes, one trainee exclaimed to me, 'It works like magic!' Professional psychologists I supervise also use the method with patients who are anxious and suffer from PTSD, with formidable outcomes. A large number of individuals suffering from the problem, who consulted me during my decades of working as a therapist, have turned their lives around for the better, ridding themselves of it in front of my very eyes. I have written this PTSD self-help book for you so that you can turn your life around and achieve similar results too.

CHAPTER 1

Understanding PTSD

PTSD known as (Post-traumatic stress disorder) is a medical condition understood. This occurs because of stress after a traumatic event, as the name suggests. Some threats a person has or can be seen can cause symptoms of post-traumatic stress disorder. The syndrome was made up of a cluster of symptoms, including hallucinations, flashes of trauma, improved irritability, and sensitivity to minor noise, sleep disorders, preventing any image or memory, which reminds the trauma patient. If these symptoms do not occur simultaneously, the person will not suffer from the post-traumatic stress disorder. Such symptoms were common in people who have experienced road accidents, natural disasters, such as earthquakes and hurricanes, fires, torture, physical and sexual violence, and war.

PTSD Treatment, Safe Alternatives

Big money is made from dealing with PTSD. In the news, Post-Traumatic Stress Disorder has become a marketing tool for all manner of medical medications, whether through services sponsored by the Federal Government or private insurers. More importantly, this form of PTSD diagnosis is based on clinical therapy, not medical science, or true human knowledge of what our military personnel and women and certain civilians suffered from. There are a few organizations, for the most humanistic approach to PTSD therapy, that focus on helping people get through the traumatic experiences and helping people build a stable, successful life for themselves.

For example, "Veterans find peace with equine therapy" was the subject of a recent channel ten news section in Sarasota, Florida, on the Circle V Ranch and rehabilitation center in Dade City. The mission of this ranch is to support veterans and first responders with alternative treatment (Alternative to the use of pharmaceutical products). The farm deals with equine therapy in order to support the veteran and the horse, and through this service, the veteran will advance throughout his life. Another counselor at the center states from the news that "they start to reconnect with each other as they interact with the horse. They will begin to communicate with the community when they connect with themselves; thus, they can start reconnecting with their families." However, the ranch offers support to the family, given that PTSD symptoms impact all.

Therapy for mental health has become the leading approach to PTSD. The FDA warns of delusions, hallucinations, mania, paranoia, suicidal thoughts, homicidal ideas, violence, and many more, which come with psychiatric medications, and for some, it involuntarily activates when a person is exposed to the adverse effects of the drugs. Staying in a psychiatric ward is an additional stigma, an additional financial burden, and another chance to diagnose and treat the patient with medications.

Dr. Gary G. Kohl has recently published a paper that is most applicable to those who have been branded Psychotic PTSD, Bipolar, Depressed, Manic, and who otherwise have been opened up for diagnosis, position on medication, and psychiatric treatment. A specialist in traumatic stress conditions, brain function, and non-pharmaceutical approaches to mental health, neuro sender disorders, food additive neurotoxicity, and psychotropic drug issues.

This benefits patients who have had adverse drug reactions have developed dependence, have symptoms of withdrawal, and/or who experience toxicity from the medications themselves. In Dr. Kohl's post, titled "Psychiatric Hospitals: On being well in 'insane areas,' if there are safety and insanity, how can we know it? "This is a popular study published in 1973 by D. L. Roshenan, which exposed the serious weaknesses of eight psychiatric hospitals at that time as professional people, like Roshenan itself, fake the symptom of hearing and admitted themselves to 12 separate psychiatric hospitals. 23 of the 41 patients were suspected by a doctor to be fraudulent, and 10 were accused of being both by a psychologist and another staff member. "From this, 41 patients were thus rescued from being diagnosed with mental illness and shielded from the altering mental effects of psychiatric drugs. Therefore, concepts of health or folly sometimes may be incorrect." Health and folly have cultural variations, for one society, what is seen as common can be seen as very aberrant in another. As just one example, there was a renowned experiment with American and British psychiatrists and diagnostic discrepancies in each region. All researchers conducted the same interviews with a psychiatric group of patients. Psychiatry was much more often treated by American physicians than by British psychiatry in this series of cases.

"Psychiatric diagnoses even erroneously convey personal, legal, and social stigmas which are impossible to shake and which often last for a lifetime." For everyone with PTSD symptoms or any other symptoms of mental health, alternative treatments are available, and medical professionals work to help you overcome this difficulty. It promises more than it was years ago. The information is available here to help you and your family gets all the facts before they decide your care. There are advocates who can help you to access this information more easily, as they, too, are committed to ensuring the right to full information.

What Are the Causes of PTSD?

In order to understand the whole theory of post-traumatic stress disorder. This is a collection of symptoms that were first described in 1860–1865, American Civil War. Physicians began noticing signs on both sides of the conflict that stopped veterans from re-entering civilian life. Some of the symptoms were serious hallucinations, usually related to noises and battle memories. Many veterans have suffered panic attacks that we now consider to be some things that would trigger battle memories, like a gunshot or a snapshot like a twig—and it would trigger PTSD. The symptoms of PTSD have been more widely recognized over the years since the Civil War. During World War I, for example, it was noticed that veterans returning from War during Europe seemed to be transformed in such a way that the people on the front door could not understand. This state was called shell shock. By the time of World War II, the army knew more than well the origins of PTSD and began working on treatment methods.

Nevertheless, post-traumatic stress disorder is not limited to soldiers alone. Anyone who has had an incident of a deep emotional wound in their life will develop PTSD symptoms. For example, a woman who has been raped might experience symptoms; if she is around strange men, or if she walks in a dark corridor, she might have panic attacks, which are identical to where her attack took place. People who have experienced a major natural disaster may also have symptoms of PTSD. Earthquake victims, for instance, can be intense fear if anything shakes the world, whether it is just as innocent as a street steamroller or a real earthquake. PTSD can also be caused by car accidents or by a violent attack on someone else. Doctors confirmed that small children who underwent surgery had experienced PTSD symptoms subsequently. Similarly, people with gunshot wounds may experience PTSD symptoms.

It is also important to note that not everybody with a significant traumatic event experiences PTSD symptoms. It is encouraging to know that there are new treatments available for those who have developed symptoms of PTSD that, in most cases, show remarkable results and enable the sufferer to return to the appearance of normal life. There is hope for those who suffer from the sometimes worsening condition—life can again be nice, and you can feel normal.

CHAPTER 2

Symptoms of CPTSD

The symptoms of PTSD are divided into four categories that are used in determining a diagnosis:

- Re-experiencing/Reliving the event
- Avoidance behaviors
- Negative mood/thoughts/feelings
- Hyperarousal (feeling on edge constantly)

We will now look further into each of those.

Symptoms of reliving an event include bad dreams, frightening thoughts, bad memories, and even flashbacks. A flashback feels like you are going through that same terrible trauma again. You relive what you believed was over and done within the past. You experience the pain over and over again, and you have no ability to stop this from occurring. Imagine being severely harmed once, but people with PTSD will have that experience multiple times. The trauma just keeps reoccurring in their minds and traumatizes the victim repeatedly, leaving the sufferer defenseless.

People with PTSD may avoid all situations that remind them of the traumatic experience. They may elude situations that may "trigger" reactive symptoms. They may stay away from the place that the situation occurred. They may stay away from the type of event that the trauma occurred. They have been known to avoid familiar situations because it brings back the horrible memories of the past experience. Avoidance can cause major upsets in a person's life. They may even be afraid to leave their home and go to work. They may isolate themselves, in an attempt, to stop themselves from being hurt again. They may also make attempts to dodge thinking, feeling, and talking about the incident altogether.

People who experience trauma may begin to think differently about themselves and those around them. They may take a more negative approach to life. Their feelings, moods, and thoughts may all suffer. They may experience feelings of guilt, shame, and mistrust. They may feel, and even believe, that the entire world is evil and dangerous. They might feel numb and lose interest in activities they used to enjoy. Or they may "block out" the situation altogether, like selective amnesia. They use this as an unhealthy way to cope with their emotional pain.

Hyperarousal is when a person is easily "startled." Their reactions are too extreme for the given occurrence. They overreact to things that do not require that type of response. For instance, jumping up every time when the phone rings. This is in response to the crisis. If you had been getting threatening calls in the past, every time the phone rings, you may feel on edge and even scared. You may have difficulty sleeping and may have outbursts of anger and even rage. Having hyperarousal symptoms may make it impossible to do daily tasks like concentrating or just taking care of yourself.

PTSD may also be present and co-occurring with other conditions such as depression, anxiety, and addiction, amongst others.

Causes and Risk Factors of PTSD

As I have already explained, the cause of PTSD is a trauma that is not appropriately dealt with. This can be a rape, torture, natural disaster, any form of violence, or a situation that caused or could have caused physical harm or death to an individual. Loved ones can also get PTSD after learning about the traumatic event.

Basically, anyone can get PTSD. Seven to eight percent of people will experience PTSD during their lifetime. Research has found that your genes may affect whether you are more prone to PTSD.

Risk factors may include experiencing past traumatic events, getting physically hurt, being a part of a violent situation, seeing another individual being harmed or killed, having a history of being abused as a child, feeling helplessness and hopeless, having no social support network in place, dealing with any additional stress in the aftermath of the trauma (rebuilding your life, healing, and getting back to normal) and having a history of other mental illnesses, or a substance abuse problem.

It is very important to remember that if you do develop PTSD that it is not your fault. You are in no way to blame. You are not weak-minded, and you did nothing to deserve the trauma. You cannot go back and stop the situation from ever occurring. But you can, and you should fight to get your life back. You can learn new coping skills and believe it or not, you can turn this terrible and very tragic experience into something positive. Instead of seeing the negative, train your mind to find the positive. And yes, there is positive in every situation. You will be tested. You will falter. But please do not give up. I have been through it too. I understand. I have empathy for you.

How to cope with PTSD

I will explore coping strategies that I have personally used to help me, and coping tips that I have found effective that others have used. I recommend you use a variety of them, not yet one or two. If, at all possible, please do use them all in your recovery from PTSD.

Admit that you have a problem. If you do not believe a problem exists, then you will feel you do not need a solution. By admitting that something is wrong (or at least could be), you will allow yourself the freedom to seek out answers. You will also unlock opportunities to get your life back on track.

Educate yourself. Reading up, researching, watching videos, etc. will allow you to gain the necessary knowledge you will need in your recovery. It will also help you to end the stigma against those with mental illness, including yourself. In addition, it will allow you to accept your illness for what it is: an illness. Knowledge is power, my friend!

Get involved by joining a support group, helping a neighbor in need, doing a kind act for someone else who is less fortunate, or volunteering somewhere. This will allow you to feel connected to those around you, build your social support network, and see life from a very different perspective.

Finding ways that help you relax is very important in those frightening situations such as nightmares, flashbacks, and events that trigger your symptoms. There are many ways to relax, and a person should use those that are most helpful to themselves, including, but not limited to, deep breathing, meditation, praying, aromatherapy, listening to calming music, taking a bubble bath, spending time with a pet, and even engaging in certain types of exercise such as yoga.

Distracting yourself. When triggering situations arise and you are unable to appropriately deal with them at that moment, it is important to try to distract yourself. Instead of thinking negativity, try thinking or doing something that you love to do, like reading a book or turn up the music. By distracting yourself, you are giving yourself a break and that is ok!

Accept the trauma for what it is and for what it's not. The situation you went through was incredibly frightening, distressing, painful, and even torturous. But you were strong enough to pull through it. You are a warrior! You had the strength required to overcome the situation. There is no need to think about it any longer, and no need to dwell on the emotional agony. What good will that do? The trauma was not your fault. It happened. Things happen, and you are not to blame. Please choose to let it strengthen you and not break you! When your mind brings you back to this terrible, tragic memory, stop it from taking control of your feelings and emotions. You are in control, and you will not let this adversity ruin you.

Sleep well. Since PTSD can cause bad dreams and nightmares related to the traumatic event, it is important to remember these tips if you are having trouble with your sleep. If a nightmare awakes you, remember that it is not really happening. It is just a bad dream. Play some relaxing music and talk to someone until you are able to fall back asleep. Also, try not to oversleep and keep on a regular sleep routine. If your nightmares continue, you may need to see a doctor who may be able to prescribe a medication designed for that.

Avoid illegal drugs, tobacco, alcohol, and caffeine. These substances will only aggravate your symptoms and will increase their intensity and occurrence. They may also affect your ability to sleep well. If you have an addiction problem, I encourage you to seek treatment for that as well.

Maintain a positive frame of mind. Life has enough negatives in it every day. There is simply no room to hold on to your negative thoughts about past events. Try letting go. Try cleansing your mind and ridding it of these negative thoughts. Replace them with positive things such as daily affirmations, prayers, inspirational sayings, and motivational quotes. Be positive and your mind will love you. Instead of seeing the negative side of everything, look for the positivity in even the worst of times. Tell yourself it will all be ok. Have hope for a brighter and better future. Allow yourself to see the opportunities and doors that will be opened to you in the future. Let go of the past and cling to the hope of what will be, not what was.

Keep the faith. In the worst of times, we need to keep the faith! Never lose faith in yourself and who you are and who you want to become. You can be your own best friend. You can be incredibly good for yourself. It is you that has limitless prospects for yourself. Never give up on you. Also, if you believe in God, remember that it is He who loves you and put you on this Earth for a reason. You must find hope in that it is He who has a miraculous plan for your life. Things may go wrong, but it is all part of a larger plan, that we may never be able to understand but must embrace. Embracing this will allow you to find peace within yourself.

Seek out a therapist, counselor, or psychologist. Preferably one who practices trauma-focused psychotherapy. Other therapies used include cognitive-behavioral therapy (CBT) and Eye movement desensitization and reprocessing. A therapist will help bring the pain to the surface. Once you are able to speak about it and vent all your feelings, you can then begin to heal the pain. You can learn to think differently about what happened. Basically, you will learn to accept it, let it go, and move forward with your life. Ultimately, it is what it is.

Find a doctor. You can look up doctors on the internet or have your primary physician refer you to a psychiatrist. This type of doctor will evaluate your case and determine if medication would be able to help you in your recovery process. Certain antidepressants are thought to be very effective in treating PTSD. The medications work on your brain chemistry, which helps stabilize your thoughts, moods, and behaviors.

If you follow all these recommendations, tips, and guidelines, you will be on your way to a very successful recovery from your PTSD!

CHAPTER 3

PTSD Symptoms Differential Diagnosis

A serious mental illness that affects not just veterans and soldiers, but also many people who are affected by or witnessed abuse or violence, is the posttraumatic stress disorder (PTSD).

While the symptoms of PTSD may seem similar to those of other disorders, there are significant and significant differences. PTSD, for example, may seem like anxiety-related symptoms, including acute stress disorder, phobia, or obsessive-compulsive disorder. In general, however, there is usually no traumatic event to cause the anxiety or worry in anxiety disorders. Or in the case of phobias, this trigger is not experienced by most people as a cause of anxiety.

The symptoms of acute stress disruption generally have to occur within a month of a traumatic occurrence and end within a month. When symptoms last longer than one month and follow other types of PTSD, the diagnosis of a person could change from acute stress disorder to PTSD.

Although there are recurrent, repetitive thoughts as a symptom for both PTSD and obsessive-compulsive disorder (OCD), the thought-forms are one way to discern these conditions. Thoughts in obsessive-compulsive disorder usually do not relate to a traumatic event in the past. With PTSD, the thoughts are invariably linked to a traumatic event in the past.

PTSD symptoms may also tend to be an adjustment disorder because they are both related to anxiety following stressor exposure. The stressor is a stressful condition for PTSD. The stressor shouldn't be severe or beyond the "normal" human experience with adjustment disorder.

The arousal and dissociative symptoms of panic disorder are typically not present in PTSD. PTSD is not a common anxiety disorder in that it is directly linked to traumatic events (it is not in generalized anxiety disorder) to avoidance, irritability, and anxiety.

Whereas a person suffering from PTSD may also be depressed, typically PTSD symptom precedes the depression (in a person with posttraumatic stress disorder, it may help to explain these depressing feelings).

In summary, a person's exposure to actual or imminent death, severe injury, or sexual assault with recurred intrusive symptoms specifically associated with this traumatic event can define post-traumatic stress disorder. After the trauma occurred, a person persistently avoided stimuli associated with the trauma and experiences major mood and thinking changes as a result of the trauma.

Anxiety Disorder Compared to PTSD

It could be a challenge to determine the difference between PTSD and other traumatic stress disorders. This dilemma is compounded by the fact that PTSD and other anxiety disorders, including GAD, often occur together. Learn how the two differ, so you can learn how the healing process starts.

Generalized Anxiety Disorder Signs and Diagnosis

Excessive worry and anxiety characterize GAD. Although most people have some worries or anxieties in their lives, someone with GAD is more concerned and anxious than it is.

The following may also happen to him or her:

- Relaxed or on the brink
- Easy to feel fatigued
- Concentration issues

- Faultlessness
- Tension of the muscle
- Disorders of the sleep pattern

GAD differs from other anxiety disorders in that GAD symptoms must occur at least six months before a disorder is diagnosed. "GAD affected 6.8 million adult people, or 3.1 percent of the U.S. population, in every given year," the Anxiety and Depression Association of the USA shared 1. If you are facing GAD symptoms, don't fight it alone.

Symptoms of Post-Traumatic Stress

PTSD is an anxiety disorder that can develop traumatic events after an individual experience. You might be frightened, desperate, or helpless. Symptoms of PTSD may begin to interfere with your daily life. The following may contain these symptoms:

- Disturbances of sleep pattern
- Faultlessness
- Outbreaks of anger
- Concentration difficulty
- Oversight
- Felt sprung or scared

You will also continue to relive the trauma. People with PTSD will experience the following trauma again:

- Returns.
- Halluces.
- Dreams of bad things.
- Mental or physiological distress.

These can be derived from mental images, ideas, and sensations. Real events, locations, or objects may cause them. Those who have difficulties with PTSD may try to avoid symptoms by avoiding trauma-related stimuli.

This prevention can be as follows:

- You or a loved one do not want to talk, think, or feel about trauma.
- You can prevent trauma-reminiscent locations, events, and individuals.
- You may not be able to remember events or an specific event.
- You could lose interest in things that you once cared for.
- You can feel unconnected.
- You may feel or appear blunt in your emotion.
- You can find it difficult to envision a perfect future, a good existence, or a normal life.

Symptoms of PTSD may feel debilitating, but they don't have to keep your life under control. How to manage your PTSD can be learned? Professional treatment, medication and speech therapy provide genuine syndrome relief, explains the National Institute of Mental Health.2

Discussing GAD and PTSD

Many symptoms overlap with GAD and PTSD. GAD is characterized, for instance, by considerable anxiety and concern. These are also problems that can arise when a person struggles with PTSD. With either question of mental health, people will prevent locations, events, and individuals from being concerned and worried.

In addition, there can be two concerns about mental health. Co-occurrence may occur because of the characteristics of one disorder as the risk factors for the other. A person who has GAD issues and then a traumatic incident may experience PTSD symptoms more likely. This has a propensity to undue worry and distress, which can be exacerbated by a traumatic event.

The connection between PTSD and Headaches

Few talks of this, but there is reason to believe there is frequent co-occurrence of post-traumatic stress disorder (PTSD). Although the attention of mental health professionals is much lower than other PTSD problems, the connection between PTSD and headaches is meaningful. If you have PTSD, you are more likely to develop various physical conditions, including diabetes, obesity, heart disease, and pain. For example, 20-30% of people with PTSD reported problems with anxiety when it came to grief in particular.

Patients with migraine or anxiety, headaches show elevated exposure to stressful events when it comes to problems. Furthermore, approximately 17 percent have PTSD diagnosed symptoms.

Another study revealed that 32 percent of OEF / OIF PTSD veterans say they have headaches problems.

The PTSD / Headaches connection

Why people with PTSD may experience problems with headaches is not entirely clear. Stress was, therefore, related to headaches, and PTSD symptoms would lead certainly to very high pressures and emotional stress. Moreover, in their daily lives, headache patients tend to experience more stressful events. PTSD can interfere significantly with many aspects and relationships of a person's life. This potentially creates more pain, which raises the risk of headaches.

In some instances, a person with PTSD may suffer from stressful experiences that may increase the risk of headaches. You may be more likely to experience headaches problems when, for example, you were in an accident or situation when you had a head injury or a traumatic brain injury. OEF / OIF-veterans have high rates of traumatic brain injuries that can take into account the number of OEF / OIF-veterans with PTSD reported headaches.

CHAPTER 4

Strategies to Recovery

Creative Strategies

Tapping into your creative side can be an effective means for processing and overcoming the after-effects of a traumatic experience. Strategies such as art, music, and writing are all viable options for trauma recovery. These creative options can be particularly useful for individuals who struggle with verbal expressions of their experiences.

Art Therapy

The therapeutic benefits of art can come from many different forms in several different settings. This can be painting, drawing, coloring, quilting, or collage with or without the direction of an art therapist, with a group or alone. A researcher who interviewed a group of art therapists was able to compile a list of the common benefits that accompany art as a recovery tool, including decreases in hypervigilance, stimulated positive emotions, and decreased anxiety.

As mentioned already, art allows for the nonverbal expression of trauma experiences and memories. It can be difficult to access the memory or find the words to express it, but art can be an effective outlet. Creating art can be a means to externalize the internal memory and own it, which helps integrate the experience as a past memory as opposed to a current source of distress.

Art can be a way to slowly gain exposure to troubling stimuli related to trauma (similar to the titration method). This non-verbal method is seen as less threatening and can make it easier to address the issues. The use of art is relaxing and reduces hypervigilance, whether or not the art is related to the trauma. Art therapy also awakens emotion so it can stimulate emotional numbing, including positive emotion. The process of creating can help in stirring and experiencing positive emotion. The creation of art can also enhance a sense of control due to the control over your creative space, which can also enhance confidence in the ability to express emotions.

One study examined the effects of coloring on anxiety. The authors found that groups coloring a detailed design, such as a mandala, saw anxiety decrease to a level that was lower than the initial measure of anxiety taken at the beginning of the study. It is interesting to note that there was no decrease in anxiety for those who were coloring the free-form of a blank piece of paper. It is believed that coloring on a design, like the one from a coloring book, helps to organize the internal chaos characteristic of anxiety. Interestingly, in the Holotropic Breathwork mentioned earlier, this type of artistic expression is often incorporated. At the end of therapy sessions involving Holotropic Breathwork, users will paint mandalas as a way to express their experiences. There are numerous coloring books available in-store and online, some full of mandalas and some that are specifically for relaxation.

A study of teenagers with high scores on a PTSD scale showed improvement in PTSD symptoms after completing art therapy. There were several art modalities used in this study, and the most effective was creating a book of artwork that contains a graphic narrative of each person's life story. Each book was made up of 13 collages or drawings along with a handmade book cover. Other specific art activities that were found to reduce symptoms of PTSD successfully include sewing pillows, beading jewelry, making ceramics, creating plaques, stitching leather purses, and decorations for holidays or seasons. Supplies and ideas for these art projects and so many more can be found at local crafting stores, and inspiration can be found online.

Music

Music is used frequently in movies, television, and even commercials to influence, signal, or alter our moods. Chances are you have used music to reflect or enhance your current mood or state of mind. Now science is demonstrating how music can regulate mood and be used to cope. Music therapy allows individuals who have survived trauma to relate to the healthy versions of themselves and can create the feeling of a safe and enjoyable environment. Music can be another source for grounding and can make traumatic memories accessible for discussion and processing. Similar to creating art, making music can create a sense of control and a means to express the trauma. Music can allow individuals to connect with and express feelings, as well as to connect with others, especially through group music therapy. Hypervigilance can also be addressed in this way by encouraging tolerance of loud sounds or silence, as well as concentration through devoting attention to music made by yourself or others.

One example is using loud drumming to express anger or using songs to lower anxiety. Specifically, anxiety-reducing songs are usually slow-paced and have an even rhythm. In more advanced versions of music therapy through the assistance of a music therapist, survivors can write and record music that creates an auditory narrative of the traumatic experience or the life story, similar to the art project mentioned earlier.

A research study conducted with a group of adults with PTSD that did not respond to cognitive behavior therapy were given 10 weeks of music therapy in which they were encouraged to improvise music with a variety of easy to use instruments (like a tambourine) while accompanied by a music therapist providing instrumental support. After the 10-week treatment period, there was a significant reduction in PTSD symptoms. Interviews with the study participants revealed that many of them felt they were able to get out their anger and frustrations through the music they produced, and afterward felt calm and controlled.

Writing

The process of writing can be a powerful tool for creative and self-expression, as well as putting words to and dealing with trauma and other intense emotional experiences. There are several benefits that come from writing, including being able to disconnect a feeling of distress from the memories of trauma, creating a sense of control and emotion regulation, and better health and well-being. It is believed that these health benefits are seen because of the decrease in inhibition through the disclosure of associated events through writing. Writing also creates the opportunity to make meaning of the traumatic event or to incorporate the event into existing ways of making meaning about the world—in other words, to help create meaning about your traumatic event that fits with your beliefs and value systems. Asking people to write on a daily basis about their traumatic experience, and the attached emotions, in particular, have been found to be especially beneficial.

In one study with college students, participants were asked to write for 20 minutes about the most traumatic and upsetting experience of their lives. After this period of writing, the students reported that the event seemed more within their control and less threatening than it had before the writing task. They also found the event to be less stressful in the present and not as central to their lives. These are all very adaptive changes in perception and have an impact on levels of distress. The students also found they had fewer intrusive thoughts and less avoidance of the memory of the situation they wrote about. This relates to less cognitive processing of the event, which means cognitive (thought) resources are more freed-up for other high-order thinking.

Other potential benefits that come from disclosing traumatic experiences, such as through the writing process, including feeling better about the topic as well as about themselves and being able to think about their situation in different ways. Writing can also lead to new and greater insight about the traumatic event, as well as less intrusive thoughts, and more self-esteem.

Trauma survivors have also reported that the process of writing about their experience helped them regain their own independent functioning and afforded them the opportunity to tell their own story. Writing is not just restricted to the standard narrative form; songwriting has also been shown to be beneficial and can be a way to combine writing and music therapy.

Another study has shown that reading and writing together can be a powerful combination. Domestic violence counselors experiencing secondary PTSD were given poems on three different occasions and instructed to reflect on the emotional theme of the poem. All the emotions of the selected poems are emotions typical of PTSD reactions and used to promote writing that is focused on personal stress and the emotions that go along with that. Participants in the study showed a decrease in symptoms and a reduction in stress.

The poems used in this study are The Armful by Robert Frost, Autobiography in "Five Short Chapters" by Portia Nelson and The Journey by Mary Oliver. These are the most frequently used poems in poetry therapy and reflect a range of emotions. You could select one or all of these poems, and after reading, write a reflection about the emotion(s) felt throughout the poem and write about that emotion(s) as they relate to your own situation.

Animal Assistance

Significant evidence has come to light about the role animals play in human lives and the benefits which can be extracted from these relationships. Many of the benefits found in human to human support relationships can also be found between humans and animals. Animals can provide a buffer between humans and challenging or threatening circumstances like trauma. It may be important to note when using animal-assisted therapy or utilizing animals for the management of trauma recovery, a human's relationship with animals is affected by their perceptions that come from media, folklore, and societal and past interactions with animals. With this in mind, animal-assisted therapies may not be for everyone.

If being around animals is for you, there are several positive benefits such as lower depression levels, better blood pressure, and the kind of physical contact that helps with the healing and recovery process from trauma. The presence of a companion animal can reduce anxiety and, in particular, can create a sense of safety during the process of disclosure during psychotherapy. Companion animals can also provide comfort and grounding as situations become difficult.

Equine Therapy

Equine, or horse therapy, is one specific kind of animal-assisted therapy that has been gaining in popularity with over 550 therapeutic riding programs available in North America and at least 3,200 registered therapeutic riding practitioners. The sensitivity and responsiveness of horses can empower riders to meet the challenges of trauma recovery.

Horses are used for therapeutic purposes because they are cooperative, patient, willing, receptive, and people-oriented. Horses can understand or "read" people and communicate with riders. This and the rider communication with the horse creates a connection that contributes to the healing process. Riding provides comfort through contact.

Part of what makes the relationship between horse and human so powerful in the process of recovering from trauma is how closely this relationship mirrors that of the relationship between a therapist and a client, also known as the therapeutic alliance. In both cases, there is a bond that reinforces a sense of self and provides a motivation to change.

It is important for a horse and rider to be matched depending on the preferences, characteristics, and personalities of both. And it takes time for the animal-human relationship to form, also very similar to the therapeutic alliance. This time can create a safe relationship and safe touch, which is very important for survivors of trauma. This safe relationship can facilitate change, as well as provide a context for goal-setting and promote a feeling of independence.

CHAPTER 5

Dialectal Behavior Therapy

In short, Dialectical behavior therapy or DBT is a form of behavioral therapy introduced by Dr. Marsha Lineham, an American psychologist who found CBT as a therapy inefficient to help people with suicidal tendencies. The foundation of this therapy utilizes the basic concepts of the standard CBT but with additional adaptations to meet the particular needs of people experiencing intense emotions. The basic aim of DBT is to empower you to manage difficult emotions by experiencing, recognizing, and accepting them. As you learn how to accept and control our emotions, you are better able to get over the harmful behaviors. To attain this goal, DBT therapists utilize a balance of change and acceptance techniques, something that is missing in other therapies meant for treating behavioral problems.

In DBT, therapists help you find the perfect balance between acceptance and change via four different elements:

- Skills training (in groups)
- Individual therapy
- Telephonic coaching
- Consultation group of therapists

A typical course of DBT includes homework and take-home assignments, which usually continue for approximately a year. A lot of people may find it quite hard to develop DBT skills in the beginning because it includes accepting your flaws while working hard to change them. However, with the passage of time, you will come to realize that all your efforts were worthwhile.

Summary

If you are living with an anxiety disorder, you most likely acknowledge that feeling in control of yourself is a validating, valuable feeling. DBT can help you achieve this feeling though group skills training, trained therapists, and skills coaching. All these parts will work together to make sure that DBT offers you skills that you can put into practice to help you get full control over how you feel and live. DBT is currently operating on four different levels—Mindfulness, Interpersonal Effectiveness, Distress Tolerance, and

Emotional Regulation—to help people get over their worst fears and depressive states.

DBT Distress Tolerance and Mindfulness Skills

Now that the concept of DBT is clear, let's move on to discuss the first two components of DBT—Mindfulness and Distress Tolerance and their role in the treatment of behavioral disorders.

What are DBT Mindfulness Skills?

Mindfulness refers to paying attention to what is happening at the moment "on purpose." When you are practicing mindfulness, you are focusing your attention on the present experience, noticing whatever is happening at the exact moment, not lost in the past, or wondering about the future.

Mindfulness is actually something entirely opposite to being on automatic pilot. While you are on automatic pilot, you are either doing things out of habit or by rote. For example, many people relate to a condition where they arrive at work but do not really remember the car ride that took you there. That is because you did not have to think about opening the car door, sitting down, putting the key in the ignition, etc. You just did all these things automatically and found yourself at your office minutes later. Doing things in an autopilot mode is not bad. It is actually quite useful in a way that helps save energy and time. Problems begin to arise when you start living most of your life in this mode instead of actually being present in the moment.

Why Does Mindfulness Matter?

Mindfulness is like a magic ingredient that helps you control your sentiments and take a step back from intense emotions. When you take a step back and notice what is happening, you are less likely to experience out-of-control emotions.

"Mindfulness is powerful."

When you use mindfulness to control your attention, you open yourself to a whole new world of choice. You do not need to act and react out of fear, habit, or intense emotions. The benefits of mindfulness have been well-researched, especially during the last few years. The regular practice of mindfulness has been shown to decrease distraction, increase emotional regulation, improve anger management, and decrease depression.

Mindfulness in DBT

Mindfulness forms the backbone of DBT. It is, in fact, the first skill taught to the patients opting for DBT. This is because, without mindfulness, it is not possible to alter long-standing patterns of acting, thinking, and feeling.

"Mindfulness is the core skill underlying all other skill sets in DBT."

It is central to getting through difficult situations, resolving interpersonal conflicts, and regulating emotions. Mindfulness is also a primary component for accessing your Wise Mind, an important foundational concept in DBT. Wise Mind is said to be the synthesis of a Reasonable Mind and an Emotion Mind. Once you find your Wise Mind, it gets easier to know what's real for you and act according to it. The concept of mindfulness in DBT revolves around two questions: "What to do" and "how to do it." These are known as the 'What' and 'How' skills.

The 'What' Skills

There are three skills that comprise the "What" of mindfulness:

- Observe
- Describe
- Participate

The Observe Skill

Observe means noticing any direct sensory experience. It is what you fee, see, taste, sense, hear, and touch without judging it, labeling it, or reacting to it. This is a bit tricky for most of the people at first; your mind wants to label what is happening around you instead of just being with the sensations of an experience. While you practice the Observe skills, you are permitting your immediate experience to happen without trying to change it or pushing it away.

Like all the skills, observe skills is experiential. This indicates that the intellectual understanding of this skill is not sufficient; you have to experience it for yourself to truly understand it. For example, listening to the sounds around you, just noticing them without passing any comments is an example of observing skill of mindfulness in DBT.

The Describe Skill

The describe skills build on the observe skill. While observe is only bare-bones attention—noticing something without adding a label or a story—describe includes putting the observed experience into words, whether it is an emotion, thought, or a sensation.

Sounds like a piece of cake, right? Not quite.

The tricky part is that DBT mindfulness demands you to practice the describe skill by sticking to the facts and refraining from any personal assumptions or interpretations. So when you describe an experience, you label thoughts as thoughts, feelings as feelings, and emotions as emotions only without adding any labels, judgments, concepts, and opinions.

The describe skill is an excellent tool to help you NOT mistake every thought or feeling of yours for a fact. For example, just because you are feeling unlovable doesn't justify it as the truth. The describe skill is also a great tool for reducing reactivity, especially in emotionally sensitive people. It does not let you jump to conclusions without checking the facts hence, saves you from a lot of trouble.

The Participate Skill

In DBT, participate means exactly what it sounds like: It means throwing yourself entirely into an activity and letting go of judgments, fear, and self-conscious instead of sitting aside and watching. Most of the young children exhibit this skill, immersing themselves in play without any sort of inhibition. For example, you can practice this mindfulness skill during everyday activities, for example, washing dishes. Instead of thinking about how much you hate it or planning what you will do once you are finished, you immerse yourself completely in the ongoing activity of washing dishes.

The 'How' Skills

The purpose of 'How' skills in DBT is to understand how to accomplish the 'What' skills. So you are supposed to practice the three 'What' skills:

One-mindfully

This means giving your full presence in the current situation, not lost in the thoughts of the past or future.

It means concentrating on one task at a time while focusing on it completely instead of splitting it between things, for example: Having a conversation on the phone while cooking a meal.

Practicing this skill is important. One-mindfulness in DBT helps you open up to the potential beauty hidden in small moments. It prevents you from juggling multiple tasks because multitasking can weaken your connection with the Wise Mind, therefore, affect your decision-making skills.

Non-judgmentally

It is common to notice something and release judgments instantly, either about yourself ("I am not good at this!"), others ("He is not good at this"), your experience ("This was indeed a bad idea"), or anything else. Most of the use judge habitually, automatically, and continuously.

Judging has become such an important part of our internal dialogue that we fail to notice how judgments can increase emotional pain and potentially destroy relationships. Hence, the 'How' mindfulness skills in DBT require you do everything non-judgmentally. Being non-judgmental prevents the emotional charge of the situation from heightening, making it easier to look for solutions.

Effectively

This skill involves acting effectively, i.e., doing what works vs. sitting aside and wishing things were different. In DBT, effectively is all about shifting your focus away from the concepts of what's fair and unfair, or who is right or wrong, and focusing on what really works. When you are not concentrated on doing what is effective, you may act in ways that are more about proving a point or being right. Trying to be right gets in the way of getting what you need or want.

CHAPTER 6

PTSD and Relaxation

Generally speaking, a relaxation technique helps a person to relax by reducing his or her level of pain, anxiety, stress, or anger, thus benefiting also from depression, headache, high blood pressure, and insomnia. In so doing, not only symptoms and/or conditions may become more manageable, but also the overall state of health may improve.

Autogenic training, for instance, which was developed by the German psychiatrist Johannes Heinrich Schultz around 1932, consists of short sessions lasting an average of 15 minutes, which are supposed to be repeated on a daily basis and that through a series of visualizations aim at generating a sense of relaxation. Positions to practice Autogenic training can be freely chosen, though finding one that may encourage the person to relax and focus on visualizations, such as lying down or sitting comfortably are highly recommended. This technique can alleviate stress-related disorders caused by traumatic events.

Biofeedback, another holistic technique, by manipulating physiological functions through the use of specific devices checking "brainwaves, muscle tone, skin conductance, heart rate, and pain perception" (deCharms et al., 2005) may also play a role in the reduction of depression, anxiety and stress. Christopher deCharms, a neuroscientist and social entrepreneur, founder, and CEO of Omneuron, a life science company whose technology is a pioneer in the imaging methods, in conjunction with Stanford University School of Medicine has developed a live fMRI aiming at measuring and modifying brain functions, with the final goal being the treatment of chronic pain. This technique enables the patient to control his own pain by visually looking at his rtfMRI and checking his own reactions in real-time, and then, by changing the latter, by ultimately blocking the pathways causing pain.

In plain English, this means that by becoming aware of one's own thoughts and perceptions at the time pain is experienced, one can change that experience by switching to a new way of thinking and perceiving. In so doing, that is, by taking control over his or her own mind and body, he or she can reduce or, through further training, even eliminate the possibility of experiencing that pain again. (deCharms, R. C. (2008). This work, which is funded by the National Institute of Health, seems to be a very promising one for the treatment of chronic pain, depression, and anxiety.

Biofeedback is far from being a new method since it has been around for millennia in India and applied through **Yoga** and **Pranayama**. While Yoga, which is a philosophical system based on the practice of physical, mental and spiritual exercises aiming at reaching a full control over both the body and the mind, focuses on a series of practices and postures to accomplish this goal, Pranayama, meaning 'prana' (life force, breath) and 'ayāma' (to extend), is a yogic discipline which also originated in India and concentrates on breathing exercises. The assumption of the latter is that since breathing is absolutely a necessity for the life of any living being, learning how to breathe properly and deeply can highly improve the health of the individual by strengthening the life force animating his or her body.

Furthermore, breathing is also seen as "the main link between conscious and unconscious," which implies that breathing properly is not only beneficial to our physical but also to our emotional and mental health. (Stanway, 1994, p. 286) Research has shown that Pranayāma can be helpful in cases of stress-related disorders. It is strongly recommended, however, to practice this kind of breathing exercises under the supervision of a qualified practitioner in order to avoid complications, injuries, and undesired side effects. (Iyengar, 2011).

As for Yoga, it focuses on maintaining a state of mind-body-spirit balance and on correcting any imbalance before it can harm the body. **Hatha Yoga** is the kind of Yoga mainly based on physical exercises, which include stretching, breathing, and relaxation. Yoga sees "the body as a vehicle, the mind as its driver and the soul as the Man's true identity" (Stenway, 1994, p. 284), hence, it can be employed to "prevent, cure and manage a variety of disorders (including respiratory, digestive, musculoskeletal and neurological ones)." It can also be an effective method to rehabilitate people after they have gone through surgeries and accidents, to manage disabilities, and to treat addictions. Yoga aims at the removal of energy (life force, prana, chi, qi) blockage through the Asana or postures, and Pranayāma, or breathing exercises, both of which are able to help the body to detoxify so that the prana may freely flow throughout it as it is intended to and maintain and/or restore homeostasis, that is the state of balance needed in order for the body to reach optimum health. All body parts can benefit from the Asanas due to the fact that through them muscles are stretched and tuned up, the spine and joints can maintain their flexibility, and breathing and circulation can be improved. (p. 285)

Although rooted in ancient Chinese philosophy and medicine and also conceived as martial arts, **Qi Gong** and **Tai Chi** (the latter also called Tai Chi Chuan) are holistic methodologies characterized by coordinated gentle postures and movements, rhythmic breathing and meditation and intended as forms of relaxation, preventive medicine, and self-healing techniques.

The benefits of both methods on health are many: They enhance the activity of the immune and lymphatic systems, of the metabolism and tissue regeneration, and increase circulation while reducing heart rate and blood pressure. Oxygenation of the brain and of all organs and tissues is also boosted and a state of relaxation is produced through the decrease of the autonomic nervous system's sympathetic response (Trivieri & Anderson, 2002, p. 435).

The health benefits of both Qi Gong and Tai Chi have also been recognized in our western world and many are now the hospitals and clinics which either recommend or have already integrated them into their practice. As for their application in cases of PTSD, these methodologies can be of great support in managing pain, depression, and anxiety.

Although relaxation alone might not be sufficient to reduce certain types of symptoms in many people affected by PTSD, it can, nonetheless, still be effective by contributing to managing the arousal associated with them.

PTSD, Nutrition, and Lifestyle

Adrenaline, cortisol and DHEA (dehydroepiandrosterone) are the hormones that help us with the 'fight-or-flight' response to stress. They intervene in the process by injecting us with the energy required to face whatever situation we encounter and perceive as a threat. This is a sort of survival mechanism which plays a fundamental role in cases of life-threatening circumstances.

However, in order to provide us with all the energies required to cope with the stressful event(s) we might be confronted with, the body takes the energies it needs from the ones reserved to perform its other functions. As a result, not only the aging process is accelerated, but there is also the possibility that many other health complications may arise. Digestive disorders or diseases, a hormonal imbalance causing the metabolism to slow down and, consequently, leading to overweight, and calcium deficiency, which may provoke arthritis, are among the many health issues that one can face in such a situation.

In order to help the body to work again towards a state of balance and possibly restore and maintain optimum health, stimulants such as coffee, cigarettes, and a high-calorie diet should be avoided. This also includes soda beverages that contain a high amount of sugar, and some kinds of sweeteners that have been proven to be toxic. Furthermore, despite the ongoing debate about the possibility, or lack thereof, that the latter might really harm human health, it seems wise, nonetheless, to limit or even to exclude these kinds of products from our diet considering, for instance, that Saccharin has been formally declared an "anticipated human carcinogen" (Day, 2007, p. 106) and Aspartame has been questioned, since it was discovered, about its potentially devastating effects on brain neurons. (p. 107).

Although a healthy and balanced diet will probably not 'cure' PTSD, the truth of the matter is that it will, nonetheless, highly contribute to the overall health and wellness by boosting one's own immune system through which the body is able to fight disease and restore health whenever required. Hence, eating plenty of fresh fruits and vegetables, with the latter being either steamed, lightly cooked or used raw, along with whole foods, 100% certified organic, good quality of proteins, better if of vegetable sources and avoiding refined, processed, saturated fat, precooked and junk foods will provide all the vitamins, minerals, enzymes your body needs to stay healthy. The B complex vitamins and vitamin C are among the very first nutrients that one should make sure to consume regularly to recover from stress, especially when the latter is intense and/or experienced over a prolonged period of time. (Holford, 2004, pp. 2018, 219)

People with mood disorders have a greater sensitivity to chemical imbalances and without a balanced diet, which may contribute to their health through the correct amount of all the nutrients the body needs, their conditions may even worsen.

The most important thing is, therefore, to develop one's own routine that can help to maximize energy and glucose levels. Good eating habits may include plenty of smoothies and/or juices (better if vegetables and fruits are combined), seeds, nuts, whole grains rather than the 'whites'—that is all processed and refined products which have been deprived of most of their nutrients—fish, chicken and or turkey while avoiding or at least consuming very little amount of meat (beef), pork, and cold cuts, while dairy products and eggs should also be consumed in moderation. Along with soda beverages also caffeine, which affects glucose levels and interferes with sleep, nicotine and illegal drugs should also be avoided. Sugar as well should be consumed moderately, for it does affect moods. Hence, cutting back on sugar, caffeine, and nicotine with the goal of completing eliminating them over a reasonable period of time, should be among the top priorities along with avoiding alcohol and drugs.

When struggling with overwhelming emotions and traumas, one might be tempted to start using either alcohol or drugs or a combination of them in order to cope with emotions and feelings, which may appear unmanageable and unbearable. In so doing, however, despite having the illusory feeling of a temporary relief, the truth is that, in the long run, all of them will backfire making the situation much worse not only in terms of PTSD symptoms but also by leading to emotional numbness and isolation along with a possible increase in anger and depression.

CHAPTER 7

What Is Psychotherapy?

Psychotherapy is, however, a conversation of a peculiar type: that is, it is both a hermeneutic and a dialectical exchange.

By hermeneutic I mean that therapists use interpretations of different kinds that prompt clients to reconsider their positions. Such interpretations may arise from the theoretical model in which the therapist was originally trained and, where this is so, it will reach back to larger discourses of different kinds—medical, scientific, therapeutic, sexual, cultural, social, and so forth. The technical device of a formulation, is, as I have explained, the device through which interpretations are presented spontaneously in a therapeutic conversation (in 'closed conversations', they may be delivered without preamble using an 'expert voice').

However, interpretations can take a looser, everyday form, and are contained in anecdotes, analogies, allusions, and suggestions, to name just a few. These informal styles have a deeper significance in that they point to the experienced therapist's facility in holding different types of conversation ranging from the theoretical, technical style at one end of the spectrum to the informal, everyday style at the other. At the same time, clients will also be using interpretations of their own, both to explain their own predicament and to interpret whatever therapists have to say to them. This to-and-from of interpretation and re-interpretation, sometimes leading to a synthesis of ideas, is what is meant by dialectic and it is this which is properly speaking, the material of psychotherapy.

However, the dialectic we find in therapy is of a peculiar kind: namely, that it is attended to subjectively by clients. Assuming that the therapist is heard to be offering them interpretations that are sincere, relevant, intelligible, and insightful (Grice, 1989: 22-40) the client will seek to apply the offering to her own life. That is to say, she will not be concerned with its objective truth so much as whether it helps her to go on in a different way (Wittgenstein, 1966: 44-45).

The texts by Wilhelm Reich and Arnold Lazarus which pointed to the 'anything-goes' quality of therapeutic interpretations and treatment choices in which those same interpretations and choices were prompted by the client sitting before them. I argued then that many experienced therapists, in practice, do not employ textbook methods in therapy but instead act as 'authentic chameleons', using all their arts of persuasion in order to bring clients round to a particular point of view or to secure their agreement to trying out a procedure on a trial-and-error basis. In my analysis of a variety of therapeutic interviews, particularly those with Gloria, I demonstrated that therapists who try too hard to impose a method on clients frequently come undone because the conversational rules of therapeutic conversations will always leave the client as the final arbiter on whether they can proceed or not. Although a minority of clients may blindly submit to indoctrination, the majority (assuming they do not misunderstand what the therapist is trying to say) will respond on a spectrum ranging from enthusiastic acceptance to outright rejection.

In the examples of therapeutic conversations analyzed so far, the formulations (interpretations) employed have sometimes been pragmatic (drawing attention to intentions and motives), sometimes theoretical (referring back to psychological theories), sometimes speculative, sometimes as an exercise of authority and occasionally as all four. Other devices have also been used in pursuit of therapeutic ends: metaphors, stories, explanations, script-formulations, tag questions, and so forth. In return, a variety of responses were elicited: angry, humorous, ironic, resistant, helpful, uninterested, perplexed, etc. Occasionally these have led to new directions in talk, but just as often they have come to a conversational dead-end. But, inescapably, the cycle of interpretation-response-reinterpretation has involved active voices constantly seeking to formulate the position from which the other is speaking. It is these continual uncertainties in interpretation which make it so difficult to analyze psychotherapy as process and outcome, or as a formal method.

Using Gadamer's work on hermeneutics, I offer a model of psychotherapy that accepts these conversational uncertainties as a given. In so doing, I seek to resolve the questions raised from the beginning of this work concerning the relationship between theory and practice and the uncertainties generated by a comparison between talk about therapy to talk in therapy. Fundamentally Gadamer helps us to understand why psychotherapy cannot ever be a formal method (i.e., a science) and why accepting and understanding that this so leads us towards an appreciation of how non-methodical (or semi-methodical) approaches can work.

CHAPTER 8

What Is Talk Cure Therapy?

It was Sigmund Freud nearly 100 years ago who came up with the term "the talking cure." Although he was referring to psychoanalysis when he initially uses the term, talking about one's problems in a safe environment with someone who is trusted, has long been shown to help with the resolution of loss, trauma, and other emotional problems.

I begin now a discussion of treatments for PTSD, starting first with a review of standard secular psychotherapies that are now commonly used to treat this disorder. Mental health professionals who provide these treatments typically have advanced degrees, are licensed by the state and received special training to administer the particular type of psychotherapy being offered. You may be surprised that current guidelines for the treatment of PTSD recommend psychotherapy over medication and all other treatments. This is based on a large volume of research showing that the benefits of psychotherapy in PTSD far exceed those of medications (and is without the side effects that medications have). Furthermore, the benefits of psychotherapy are more long-lasting than those on medication, which may help some persons only during the time that the medication is actually being taken.

Many different kinds of psychotherapies have been proposed for the treatment of PTSD. However, only a few of these have been shown in scientific studies (i.e., randomized clinical trials) to have the benefit. I will now discuss each of these below, as well as other psychological approaches to treatment that are reasonable, but have far less evidence to support their effectiveness. When discussing these various psychotherapies and psychological treatments, I will be referring to what is called an "effect size" (ES). The ES indicates the size of the clinically meaningful effect that the treatment has. In other words, the ES is a quantitative measure of the benefits that you may receive after undergoing a course of the particular type of psychotherapy. ES's that indicate a small clinical effect on reducing PTSD symptoms are those that are -0.20 or closer to 0; a moderate effect is indicated by ES's in the range of -0.30 to -0.60, and a large clinical effect or benefit is indicated by ES's in the -0.80 or more negative range. ES's also have what are called "95% confidence intervals." This is a statistical term that means 95% of people who received the therapy fall within the range of values provided. If a 95% confidence interval includes 0, then the clinical benefit of the treatment is considered to be the same as no treatment at all.

Most of the time these studies compare the psychotherapy being studied with a "control" condition where participants receive no treatment (controls might be placed on the waitlist to receive the therapy later or may simply receive "usual care," i.e., the care they would ordinarily receive if they were not in the study). On occasion, the psychotherapy being studied will be compared with other "active" treatment (such as another type of psychological treatment or medication). Of course, it is much more difficult to show a large ES (indicating a clinically meaningful difference) if psychotherapy is compared to other treatment than if it is compared to no treatment or usual care. Now that may be more information that you are interested in, but it may be helpful so that we can compare the effects of psychotherapy with medication and other treatments.

Psychotherapies currently used to treat PTSD can be divided into "trauma-focused therapies" and "non-trauma-focused therapies." I begin with the trauma-focused therapies since these are usually recommended for those with PTSD.

CHAPTER 9

What Is Cognitive Behavioral Therapy?

Cognitive Behavioral Therapy (CBT) is an approach that addresses behavioral dysfunctional emotions, and cognitive processes based on a combination of core behavioral principles and cognitive techniques. CBT is used by problem-focused and action-oriented approach practitioners to support people cope with common conditions such as fear, stress, and often more complicated psychological disorders.

Cognitive-behavioral therapy refers to a number of structured psychotherapy methods centering on the thoughts behind the problems of a patient. A survey of nearly 2,300 psychologists in the U.S. found that about 70 percent uses CBT in combination with other therapies to treat depression and fear. CBT is also a predominant paradigm of psychotherapy that is taught in graduate psychology programs.

How Does Cognitive Therapy Work?

Cognitive-behavioral therapy is based on the idea that human beings are somewhat irrational and make many illogical mistakes whenever they assess the risks and benefits of their thoughts and actions from different situations and courses. It can relate to the feelings that are out of balance, such as rage and depression. But CBT is also used to address a number of other nuanced problems, including post-traumatic stress disorder (PTSD), OCD, drug misuse, ADHD, eating disorders, bipolar disorder, and other illnesses.

For them to be successful, cognitive-behavioral clinicians will have a strong interaction with their customers, such as positive listening skills and a good personality fit. This is because the patient and therapist are working together to discuss the issues at hand and the reasons for the patient's thoughts and actions toward those issues. The end aim is to alter ways of thought such that the individual feels less consistently unpleasant mental conditions.

The Global Coalition for Behavioral Wellbeing in favor of CBT as it has outstanding research evidence promoting its application in the therapeutic diagnosis of mental illness, which has gained broad acceptance among both clinicians and patients alike. Increasing numbers of psychologists, psychiatrists, social workers, and psychiatric nurses are getting CBT training.

Research on CBT's effectiveness has been found to be effective against a wide range of disorders. Those experiments are well-controlled, the data is properly reviewed and the findings speak for themselves. Of starters, CBT has been shown to have substantial advantages when managing bipolar depression, culminating in fewer treatment days, reduced suicide rates, and decreased levels of parasuicidal or self-injurious behavior.

Precautions to be Taken before Beginning Relational Cognitive Therapy

Psychiatrists, behavioral psychologists, social workers, and other mental health professionals undergo years of training and education, but without this solid training experience, it is possible to practice counseling. Before settling on a CBT specialist, other items to study include educational background and qualifications, along with any professional associations to which they belong, such as the Organization for Behavioral and Cognitive Therapies, where most top practitioners are participants. Review your history, schooling, credential, and license before seeing a making your first appointment. The general term psychotherapist is often used. Make sure the therapist you choose meets the requirements of state certification and licensing for his or her particular discipline. The key is finding a qualified therapist who can match your needs to the type and therapy. CBT is more effective in most situations when paired with various therapies, such as taking medicine. So, you might also need a psychiatrist to prescribe medications besides your therapist.

The cost is one more thing to consider. When you have health care, find out what pays all the treatment services it provides. Some health plans cover just a certain number of sessions of therapy a year. Some may not even be covered. So, make sure to negotiate the costs and payment plans with the psychiatrist before the first meeting.

Think about what issues you're experiencing that require care when you first assign. Although you should still work some of that out with your psychiatrist, a clearer understanding of your issues will serve as a beginning point in advance. Check again for their qualifications and experience, especially with your questions. Some therapists may not meet the requisite qualifications. If first time around you don't find the right one, don't give up. Do the research, and locate a reliable Cognitive Behavioral Therapist.

Emotional Habits and CBT

It is commonly said that human beings are creatures of habit.

Typically, this definition is used in relation to our behavior—though in recent years, we have noticed that the way we think is also commonplace. Since we all realize how we think has a great deal to do with how we act, a good question to ask is, what are my emotional habits?

What Are the Emotional Habits?

Emotional habits do have two dimensions:

How we generally feel as we go about the task of living our lives, day after day.

If we react emotionally (again and again) to particular situations/events occurring in our lives.

The thoughts and emotions cannot be separated; they exist in unison during almost every moment of life. To be person, in other terms, is to be in a state of continuous thinking and feeling—and the implicit complexities of that continuing subjective experience are partly normal. Anxiety behaviors, depression, anger, irritability, helplessness, frustration, envy, fear, worry, and so on. When we constantly feel nervous and worried about what others think of us, or anxious about what our future holds, or frustrated and insecure about how our lives compete with others, it can be said that we have become used to repeating patterns. This is not to condemn oneself or minimize the impact of real-life events and situations. The point is to put us in the driver's seat and suggest that if we've been used to these habits, then we can re-accustom ourselves to them and to other / healthier trends.

Beware of the Oversimplification of CBT (Cognitive Behavioral Therapy)

CBT is of enormous benefit to people all over the world, and to the field of mental health in general. However, the oversimplified assertion that you can alter your mindset and change your life (as it happens in media sound-bites) can misinterpret the true essence and meaning of CBT and the related methods of psychotherapy it has encouraged. Why? And it means that it's quick and convenient to adjust your outlook (like adjusting your shampoo or something). This may even bring us to the mistaken assumption that the job is done because you're 'changing your mind.' That cannot be any further from the facts. To become agents of change in regard to our own ways of thinking and feeling is analogous to learning and mastering a musical instrument that I will talk to for a minute. First, another argument regarding the possibility of oversimplifying CBT. Let us look at this idea, which is often heard:

It is not what happens to us that matters the most, but how we react to what happens to us. I couldn't be more decided. However, it is crucial that we go a move forward and explain that our INITIAL response/reaction to 'stuff' is not nearly as crucial as how we reply overtime—over the course of the hour, day, week, month, and year. We might blow up, shut down, stress out, diminish, take no notice, fall down, have a heart attack, etc. Okay, great, so what are we doing THEN?

And after that, THEN... what do we do? And so forth. My point is that what matters most is not the discreet moments but the ongoing (and always imperfect) process of striving for a good living. It is important to do that because we question ourselves: Is my fundamental orientation to a life centered on constantly seeking to learn and grow from the challenges and complexities of life? Am I leading a more emotional existence of accusing someone, avoiding responsibility, and whining constantly that things are not the way I would like them to be? Changing thinking & emotional patterns is like learning to play the guitar. It's lifelong learning to become someone who can play the guitar (which I do) and I think most would agree that it's ideally pursued as a love job. The same is true in my view for learning to change our thinking and emotional habits. Yes, in our efforts to learn any musical instrument there are 'techniques' that we employ. The most critical part of studying how to play an instrument, though, is NOT the strategies or methods, nor is it the teaching system or even the teacher's standard. What counts most is the degree of enthusiasm and commitment that the student brings to the project, along with the amount of artistic practice and success he/she puts in overtime.

The Ethos of Continuous Learning and Development

We have also been born in a society riddled with social signals encouraging instant gratification and an attitude of rapid obsession. So, it's no surprise we've built an over-reliance on shortcuts, suggestions, and the "newest cutting edge" strategies. Of reality, they don't offer the goods; what really succeeds in doing something meaningful is to apply the fundamentals over and again, while actively drawing on the gradual experience and ability increases. In the school of life, the mentality of "pulling all-nights" and "cramming" for exams will not represent us well; what truly matters in this realm is a sincere and consistent dedication to ideals and activities that suit us well and others.

CHAPTER 10

What Is Cognitive Processing Therapy?

Cognitive Processing Therapy (CPT) is a therapeutic approach that targets changes in thinking that are typical following a traumatic event, including changes in the way you think about yourself and the world. The goal of CPT is to help you learn to examine your thinking and determine if there is an alternative point of view. Because of how profoundly trauma changes your thinking, a part of this work requires you to go back and revisit the traumatic event in order to understand how your current—often unhelpful—thought processes developed.

When we're exposed to information that doesn't match our view of the world, we typically do one of two things in response: We either change the information to fit our beliefs ("maybe I wasn't really raped") or we change our beliefs ("maybe bad things do happen to good people"). Sometimes, belief changes become extreme, such as thinking I always make mistakes or only bad things happen to me (which is sometimes called overgeneralization).

In CPT, the first step is to work on integrating the traumatic experience into your belief systems and memories so that you begin to come to terms with what happened. The next step is to modify any overgeneralized beliefs. Some of our emotions are biologically hardwired—like feeling fear in response to danger or sadness in response to loss—but many of our emotions, such as guilt and shame, are thought to be "manufactured" as a result of faulty thinking. The good news is manufactured emotions often dissipate following the changes in thinking CPT helps cultivate.

Cognitive tasks, including something as simple as labeling objects, activate the logical part of our brains, like the prefrontal cortex, which in turn helps regulate the emotional parts of the brain like the amygdala. Using your words to talk about and analyze the traumatic event, calms overactive emotional responses. The goal of CPT's therapeutic exercises, which we'll explore below, is to increase flexibility in your thinking and support your ability to think critically about what you've been saying to yourself about why the traumatic event happened and what it means about yourself, others, and the world around you. "Stuck points" are negative trauma-related thoughts or beliefs that are exaggerated or distorted in some way that will ultimately impede your recovery. Specifically, stuck points are the problematic ways you evaluate the traumatic event, like the common belief that if you'd acted differently, you could have kept it from happening. These beliefs could be new (post-trauma), or the trauma might have served as confirmation of some negative beliefs you already held. For instance, someone who, prior to a traumatic event, placed great trust in authority figures like the police may begin to develop a new belief that police are worthless and untrustworthy because they weren't able to respond quickly enough to prevent an assault. In contrast, someone who went through a similar scenario but already had difficulty trusting authority would confirm their long-standing beliefs following the trauma.

If you've been thinking the same things over and over again ever since your traumatic event, without reconsidering those thoughts or exploring alternative ideas, the thoughts have likely become habitual and entrenched in your beliefs. In order to begin to shift those thought patterns, you must approach your thoughts and beliefs with an open mind and a willingness to challenge your assumptions.

CPT was developed to treat a range of disorders and mental health difficulties, including PTSD, depression, anxiety, personality difficulties, problems with substance use, and difficulties surrounding self-esteem and self-concept. CPT has been heavily researched, and there is strong evidence for its effectiveness across a variety of populations. Study results indicate that participants have seen significant decreases in self-reported PTSD as well as in other trauma-related mental health difficulties, both during treatment and at six-month follow-ups.

Common Problematic Thought Patterns

Sometimes called cognitive distortions or "stinking' thinking,'" the following list of problematic thought patterns has been associated with both depression and PTSD. Learning about these patterns can help you begin to identify the thinking that may be causing you increased distress.

We all engage in distorted thinking at times, but when these thought patterns become habitual, significant emotional distress can result. Once you learn to identify the ways in which your thinking can be distorted, your goal becomes to "catch it and correct it" before the thoughts lead to negative emotions.

Magnification and Minimization: This occurs when you either exaggerate or minimize the importance of something. For example, you may discount your achievements, but become excessively focused on your mistakes.

Catastrophizing: Focusing your attention on the worst possible outcome of a situation and assuming that it is a likely possibility.

Overgeneralization: When you make a broad interpretation from one event. For example, you might think, *I felt awkward on that date. I am always so awkward.* Or, *I got the wrong answer to that question. I am always so stupid.*

Magical Thinking: Linking actions to unrelated situations. For example, believing those bad things will not happen to you because you are a good person.

Personalization: This occurs when you take things too personally or relate situations to yourself that may actually have nothing to do with you. For example, *She looks pissed off. I must have done something wrong.*

Jumping to Conclusions: Making assumptions or interpreting the meaning of a situation with little or no evidence.

Mind Reading: When you interpret the thoughts and beliefs of others without adequate evidence. *He didn't invite me to go to lunch. He probably hates me.*

Fortune-Telling: When you assume that a situation will turn out badly without adequate evidence. *I will never stop feeling this way.*

Emotional Reasoning: Assuming that your emotions reflect reality. *I feel angry; therefore, you must have treated me badly* or *I am sad, therefore, I am not going to get what I want.*

Disqualifying the Positive: Focusing only on the negative aspects of a situation while ignoring the positive aspects. For example, you may receive many compliments from your friends, but remember the single piece of negative feedback someone told you.

"Should" Statements: Fixating on beliefs that things should be a certain way. *I should be married by now. I should be happy.*

All-or-Nothing Thinking: Thinking in absolute terms, such as *always, never,* and *every: I never do anything right. I am always going to be lonely.*

CHAPTER 11

Somatic or "Right-Brain" Psychotherapy

Most forms of talk therapy focus on the left side of the brain that deals with talking and logical thought. For example, in cognitive therapy, you discuss your negative thoughts and feelings with your therapist and try to think of more positive or constructive ones. In "person-centered" counseling (the most common form of advice), you discuss your counselor's issues, and your counselor provides periodic feedback. In somatic therapy, the client shifts from exploring and analyzing their thoughts, behaviors, and personal history to focusing on their internal sensations. For example, the therapist might notice that the client looks uptight and distressed. She then asks where the client is experiencing physical tension. The client mentions the tension in their jaw and shoulders, and a feeling of irritation and anger related to a recent argument with a relative. Hence, there is a shift in mental activity from the logical, verbal, left neocortex to the right side of the brain, which is a more intuitive part of the brain that interacts more closely with the body, brain stem, and the limbic system.

A big advantage of this type of therapy is that it avoids many of the ego-clashes than often occur in traditional talk therapy. Instead of probing deeply into your personal history or situation, the main focus is on your physical sensations. It means that the therapist isn't challenging the client to change their attitude, thinking radically, or behavior. The client doesn't have to divulge lots of personal information if they don't want to. The primary requirement is to be willing to focus on your physical sensations, take note of any related thoughts or feelings. A process that tends to pique people's curiosity and can often be quite pleasant, particularly if you unlock an area of physical tension or discomfort. Another benefit of somatic therapy is it tends to be less mentally demanding that cognitive therapy, which can require a lot of mental effort and discipline on the part of the client.

Sometimes the therapist may engage in small experiments with the client, such as asking them to exaggerate a tension pattern in the shoulders, or seeing how the client reacts if they increase or decrease eye contact. As somatic psychotherapy progresses, the therapist works within the client's window of tolerance while slightly pushing their boundaries to widen their tolerance window. For example, if the client is looking relaxed during therapy, the therapist can test their comfort zone by doing role-play exercises and seeing how their body language changes when they forced to act in a way they aren't using. The client and therapist may also set specific goals, such as increasing social confidence, or increasing their ability to tolerate feelings of restlessness and boredom without resorting to drugs or alcohol. If the goal is to improve the human spirit, the focus might be on sensing their posture and tolerating unpleasant sensations in the chest and belly. If the goal is to explore feelings of sadness, body awareness might direct towards facial expressions and the head's downward tilt.

The main drawback of somatic psychotherapy is a lack of trained therapists with the skills to take full advantage of it. It can take a lot of training and experience for the therapist to know what body language cues are meaningful indicators of underlying mental stress, and which are not. Most psychologists and counselors receive very little training in somatic therapy or body awareness. Despite an increasing amount of research, somatic treatment can be useful for several stress-related disorders such as post-traumatic stress disorder. Some somatic therapists say the relative lack of interest in this form of treatment is due to cultural factors. Over the last few hundred years, western culture has tended to see the mind and body as independent of one another. Some critics, some as medical historian Edward Shorter, say this tendency has been a problem in 20th-century psychiatry, with its over-emphasis on Freudian psychotherapy in the 50s and 60s and later, by drugs aimed at correcting supposed chemical imbalances in the brain. However, the increasing popularity of eastern mind-body practices like yoga is sparking a greater interest in developing western mind-body practices that incorporate the latest scientific knowledge about the wider nervous system and its effects on the mind and body.

While somatic therapy for symptoms of anxiety and depression is yet to go mainstream, it is already quite widely used for dealing with PTSD, as well as some physical health problems, such as chronic back and nerve pain.

Where somatic psychotherapy is unavailable or unaffordable, body-based somatic therapy can combine with self-administered cognitive therapy. In self-administered cognitive therapy, as outlined in popular self-help books like David Burns' Feeling Good: The New Mood Therapy, you keep a written record of persistent negative thoughts, critique your ideas and come up with constructive responses. This basic DIY cognitive therapy approach can combine with somatic, brain-body methods, such as the following exercise suggested by Pat Ogden:

- Identify a persistent negative belief (e.g., I'm an angry person and can't do anything about it)
- Observe how your body reacts to the negative mindset (e.g., my jaw and shoulders tense up, and I can't think clearly)
- Think of a different physical movement you could make (e.g., I could clench my left hand, or shake my shoulders)
- Make the alternative movement several times
- Make a mental or written note of any improvement in your thoughts or feelings (e.g., I feel less tension in the upper body, and I don't feel quite so angry).

Self-administered cognitive therapy is quite effective for mood disorders, so there's every reason to expect some positive benefits combining self-administered cognitive therapy with body-based treatment.

A basic cognitive therapy diary is divided into three columns. In column one, you write down your beliefs and thoughts, such as "I am lazy," and in column two, you write down the mental consequences of your dreams, such as "I feel worthless." In the third column, you write down your rational responses to your negative thoughts, such as "I'm over-generalizing, I often put in a lot of effort," or "this simplistic thinking doesn't help me to feel positive or want to try harder."

CHAPTER 12

What Is EMDR?

EMDR—Eye Movement Desensitization and Reprocessing

Eye Movement Desensitization and Reprocessing or EMDR designed, and EMDR is just one of the more recent "energy" therapies which were recently recognized and accepted by the expert community and the public. They're called "power" treatments since they work much faster than conventional "talk therapy" or psychotherapy. Other hastened remedies are NET(TM), hypnosis, TFT, along with the TFT offshoots like EFT.

EMDR/Eye Movement Desensitization and Reprocessing is an alternative fast remedy that functions by targeting the core areas of the mind. Chat treatment, in contrast, concentrates primarily on the

Prefrontal Cortex and is based on insight into impact change. EMDR works mostly through the subconscious mind, although penetration often comes as an outcome.

It's speculated that EMDR also activates and immediately affects the mind/body continuum and so can be classified as an "energy conservation" too. Energy psychology is derived from Chinese medicine and more especially about the acupuncture/acupressure system. This system considers that chi, which can be energy or electricity travels throughout the meridians or rivers of acupuncture points in your human body. This energy can get jaded by bodily, psychological, or traumatic facets. Energy psychology postulates that by balancing this particular system, the issues from these types of triggers are quickly alleviated.

Eye Movement Desensitization and Reprocessing functions on several issues, but is particularly successful with traumas both present and past.

The therapist immediately moves their hands back and forth while requesting the client to move just their eyes whenever they monitor the hand movement. The client is guided to think about this injury through the process. Following 20-25 hand motions, the client is asked to concentrate on what difficulty, feeling, idea, or facet of this injury is currently most notable. The process is then repeated with this new goal. The issue is often painlessly solved after just a couple of sessions when compared with conventional treatment, which often lasts for weeks or even years.

This motion of the eyes imitates the REM or rapid eye movements, which can be created when an individual is dreaming. It's speculated that we change short-term memory to long-term memory through REM. The psychological part of long-term memory is considerably reduced and can be recalled as though from a fantastic distance. Any injury may get trapped, particularly if it's painful and acute. This sort of treatment can easily and effectively get rid of this impediment and also reprocess the info, thus relieving the issue.

Number for Clinicians

Eye Movement Desensitization and Reprocessing (EMDR) is a form of psychotherapy that was initially made to relieve the distress associated with traumatic memories. Adaptive Data Processing version posits that EMDR treatment eases the obtaining and processing of traumatic memories as well as other negative life experiences and to deliver them into a flexible resolution. After successful treatment using EMDR treatment, affective distress is alleviated, unwanted beliefs are reformulated, and bodily stimulation is diminished.

During EMDR treatment, the customer attends to mentally upsetting material in short successive doses while simultaneously focusing on an outside stimulus.

Therapist guided medial eye movements would be the most frequently used external stimulation, but various different stimuli such as hand-tapping and sound stimulation are usually utilized. EMDR therapy eases the access to this traumatic memory system, in such a way that data processing is improved, with new institutions formulated between the traumatic memory and even more elastic memories or data.

These new institutions are considered to lead to full data processing, and new understanding, elimination of psychological distress, and growth of cognitive insights. EMDR treatment employs a 3-pronged protocol:

1. The previous events which have laid the basis for importance have been processed, and hammering new associative connections with elastic advice;

2. The recent conditions that evoke distress are concentrated, and external and internal causes are desensitized;

3. Imaginary templates of potential events have been integrated, to help the customer in obtaining the skills necessary for flexible functioning.

What is EMDR?

For Laymen

EMDR (Eye Movement Desensitization and Reprocessing) is a type of psychotherapy that enables individuals to heal in the indicators and psychological distress, which would be the end result of upsetting life adventures. Repeated studies show that by employing EMDR treatment, people may experience the advantages of childbirth that took decades to make a difference. It's widely believed that acute emotional pain requires a lengthy time to cure. EMDR treatment shows that the brain can actually be cured of an emotional injury as your system recovers from bodily injury. If you cut your hand, your system functions to close the wound. When a foreign object or recurrent harm irritates the wound, then it festers and triggers pain. When the irritant is removed, recovery resumes.

EMDR treatment shows a similar sequence of events as happens with psychological processes. Your brain's information processing method obviously goes toward psychological wellness. In the event the machine is blocked or obscured from the effect of an upsetting event, the psychological wound festers and can result in extreme suffering.

When the cube is removed, recovery resumes. Employing the comprehensive protocols and processes learned in EMDR treatment training sessions, clinicians assist customers to trigger their normal healing procedures.

Over 30 positively controlled studies are performed on EMDR treatment. A few of the studies show that 84%-90% of single-trauma sufferers no longer have post-traumatic anxiety disorder after just three 90-minute sessions. Another study, financed by the HMO Kaiser Permanente, found that 100 percent of those single-trauma sufferers and 77 percent of multiple injury victims no longer have symptoms associated with PTSD after just six 50-minute sessions. In a different study, 77 percent of combat veterans were complimentary from PTSD at 12 sessions. There's been much research about EMDR treatment and it is currently considered an effective type of therapy for injury and other upsetting experiences by renowned associations like the American Psychiatric Association, the World Health Organization, and the Department of Defense. Given the global recognition as a successful way of treating injury, you will be able to readily see how EMDR treatment could be effective in curing the "regular" memories which are why people have reduced self-esteem, feelings of powerlessness, and the myriad of other issues that bring them for treatment. More than 100,000 clinicians around the globe use the treatment. Huge number of people have been treated successfully within the last 25 decades.

EMDR treatment is an eight-phase treatment. The eye

moves (or alternative bilateral stimulation) can be utilized during a portion of this session. After the clinician has decided which memory to aim, he requests the customer to hold unique facets of the event or idea in their mind and also to utilize their eyes to monitor the therapist's hands because it goes back and forth through the customer's area of vision. As this occurs, for reasons considered by a Harvard researcher to become correlated with all the biological mechanisms involved with Rapid Eye Movement (REM) sleep, inner relationships appear and the customers start to process the memory and also upsetting feelings. Ineffective EMDR treatment, the significance of debilitating events is changed on a psychological level. As an example, a rape victim changes from feeling dread and self-disgust into holding the firm belief, "I lived it, and I'm powerful. "Unlike talk treatment, the insights customers gain in EMDR treatment result not too much from clinician interpretation; but, by the customer's own hastened intellectual and psychological processes. The web impact is that customers conclude EMDR treatment feeling permitted from the most experiences that after debased them. Their wounds didn't only shut, rather they've transformed. As a consequence of this EMDR curative procedure, the customers' ideas, feelings, and behavior are robust indicators of psychological wellness and settlement—without talking in detail or doing assignments employed in different remedies.

EMDR treatment is really a phased, concentrated method of treating trauma along with other ailments by reconnecting the customer in a protected and quantified method into the pictures, self-thoughts, feelings, and body sensations connected with the injury, and enabling the natural healing powers of their mind to move toward elastic resolution. It's founded upon the premise that symptoms happen when injury and other harmful or challenging experiences interrupt the mind's natural ability to cure, and also that the recovery process can be eased and performed via brute stimulation while the customer is re-experiencing the injury from the context of a secure surrounding like their therapist's office (double awareness).

How Does EMDR Work?

During EMDR, people safely reprocess traumatic data until it's no longer emotionally disruptive to their own lives. There are just 8 stages of therapy, and at the Rapid Eye Movement stage, the person targets a tumultuous memory and explains the belief that they hold about themselves. When it's connected to the adverse memory (by way of instance, in handling abuse, the individual could think, "I deserved it") the person then formulates a favorable impression they would love to own ("I'm a rewarding and decent individual in charge of my own life "). Each of the senses and feelings that move together the memory has been recognized. The person subsequently reviews the memory whilst focusing on the external stimulus that makes bilateral eye motion. Normally this is achieved by seeing the therapist precede two hands. After every pair of bilateral moves, the person is asked how they believe. This procedure proceeds until the memory is no more upsetting to the person. The person is calculating the injury.

The chosen positive view is subsequently set up, via analog motion, to substitute the negative impression.

Sessions generally last for one hour. It's speculated that EMDR works since the "uncanny stimulation" by-passes the region of the brain that processes memories, but is now becoming trapped on account of the injury and can be preventing the mind from appropriate storage and processing of their memory. During EMDR, people process the memory and that results in a peaceful resolution leading to improved consciousness regarding both formerly disturbing event as well as also negative thoughts about themselves, which have grown from the first traumatic event.

Who Replies EMDR Treatment?

EMDR treatment has been endorsed by The American Psychiatric Association and the International Society for Traumatic Stress Research. Moreover, it's used by the United States Department of Veterans Affairs, the

Department of Defense, and abroad associations, such as the United Kingdom Department of Public Health, along with the Israeli National Council for Mental Health.

There are currently over 30 regular gold Studies documenting the efficacy of EMDR treatment within the last 30 years, having issues like rape and sexual abuse, combat injury, childhood trauma and failure, life-threatening injuries, and symptoms like stress, depression, and substance misuse.

Edy Nathan, MA, LCSW, is an accredited Psychotherapist with more than 20 years' experience and has been licensed as an EMDR practitioner, believes that this kind of treatment has the capability to cure individuals that suffer from all kinds of injury. "Exactly what the procedure does is to change how we process that the existence of the physiological, psychological, and mental effects related especially to some traumatic event," she explained. "The pain and feel of risk carried within oneself following a traumatic event grasp the soul with this kind of order it contributes to a feeling of being in emotional quicksand.

EMDR functions to interrogate perception systems, also called cognitions, which affects the negative cognition by means of a string of lateral eye movements, etc.

CHAPTER 13

Trauma and PSTD—PTSD Treatment with Hypnotherapy

Trauma is something most of us will have to deal with on our life journey at some point. Yes, it is projected that sometimes 50% to 90% of us will have to deal with it.

Psychological trauma is always a product of an experience that overwhelms the victim and does not handle or fully control the emotions produced by that experience.

The subconscious mind is disturbed by distress by an incident or a number of events, and this has profoundly affected the individual's functioning.

Essential and effective though it is certainly for the traumatized individual, the actual experience itself is less essential on a psychological level than its interpretation and reaction.

It explains why one person can very well shrug a similar event off but creates real difficulties in another. What can be a traumatic experience is not traumatic for one person.

Trauma itself can happen on a life journey at any time.

This can occur during infancy, and as a result of, for example, psychological, physical abuse, or extreme poverty and can leave the child traumatized in adulthood.

And traumas arise later in life, triggered by neglect, injuries, injury, crime, war, death, and natural disaster.

Although trauma itself is painful, about 8% are more debilitating and paralyzing effects of the Post-Traumatic Stress Disorder (PTSD) trauma.

If left untreated, PTSD can have serious consequences for the patient, serious implications, and ability to function at work or interpersonal level.

PTSD also stems from real physical damage encounters or experiences. Occasionally, however, psychological and emotional distress may cause it where no actual physical harm is involved.

Very often, though, it blends both aspects.

While a persistent and significant emotional response to trauma is essentially post-traumatic stress disorder, it differs from combat stress or traumatic stress in that it is typically much more severe and not at all transitory.

PTSD has also historically been identified as shell shock, combat tiredness, and post-traumatic stress syndrome.

Yet fighting is not sufficient to be affected by PTSD, any real trauma to the nervous system—such as a car accident or death, addiction to drugs or sexual assault—can lead to it.

However, whatever the cause, the resulting symptoms of trauma are real and distressing for a person who has to experience them.

Those with this type of trauma can experience chronic and acute anxiety, frustration, sleep disturbance, disturbing thoughts, breathtaking disorder, or nightmares. We also find it very difficult to think about trauma cases.

We find it difficult or impossible to effectively deal with and incorporate these issues on the subconscious level of the mind, owing to their upsetting nature.

And here, transformational hypnotherapy with experience can be extremely useful, offering psychological care that can lead to a full recovery from trauma.

The unconscious mind, working with a skilled and highly trained transformational hypnotherapist, can be guided to reconstitute traumatic experiences of the past in order to neutralize and reverse the damage.

The truth is that the person survived, given the frightening expectations and beliefs that were instilled during the traumatic experience. Ultimately, he or she did it through.

The details of the traumatic experience exist with the right trauma therapy, but the meaning and psychological symptoms previously induced by these facts have always been changed.

Effective trauma care allows the patient to deal with what happened so that the person can then let his or her life go and go on.

For example, leaving the traumatized person in no way means that he has to forget what has happened in the past.

Nonetheless, it very often means that an abuser or any person who has actively participated in the traumatic experience must be encouraged to forgive.

It's not for religious reasons, nor is it altruistic in any way. It's simply because failure to do so holds the person in contact with the past, retains and supports the harm the ongoing trauma pain, the continuing emotional and mental trauma.

It must be stressed that the traumatized person is encouraged to forgive. It is not necessarily the person or people who may have caused the trauma. In reality, the person or persons responsible for this very often do not know forgiveness.

But the traumatized person is released and released

through real forgiveness. The patient is shown how to forgive the past with the help of transformational hypnotherapy so as to heal and move on with their lives.

If you or someone you care about has the truly debilitating and deteriorating consequences of trauma, it can really be done.

The Benefits of Hypnotherapy as PTSD Therapy

The quality of a person's life can be severely affected by post-traumatic stress disorder (PTSD). Numerous PTSD treatments with hypnosis are one of the choices. Is hypnotherapy an appropriate way to overcome PTSD, and what does it bring about?

What is Post-Treatment Stress Disorder?

Traumatized people may feel a sense of loss, anxiety, panic, and fear. Whenever these symptoms last a very long time and tend to affect the quality of life, they are referred to as post-traumatic stress disorder.

PTSD is characterized by the re-experience of traumatic incidents and hallucinations, the inability to deal with stress, and heightened fear or anxiety. Reminders such as fast breathing, intense physical reactions, and general apathy are also typical for PTSD.

Events like War, death of a loved one, natural disasters, children's problems and abuse, kidnapping, sexual abuse, domestic violence, and aviation crashes often lead to this condition. Any other life-changing and devastating incident may also contribute to PTSD.

How can PTSD sufferers Hypnosis Aid People with PTSD be recommended to try hypnotherapy because it helps in several ways?

Many of the effects experienced by PTSD are close to what happens during the hypnotherapy. Individuals with PTSD respond to hypnosis quite well and have access to the guidance of the therapist to painful memories. These memories can be restructured by hypnosis to prevent future PTSD symptoms.

Hypnosis and self-hypnosis are also great instruments for managing PTSD recurrences.

Various studies have been conducted to test these arguments. Hypnosis treatment is at least as effective as alternative treatments for PTSD, such as psychotherapy, scientific evidence on the efficacy of hypnotherapy. A study was conducted in 2005 in order to compare hypnotherapy against other therapies widely used to relieve symptoms of PTSD. The findings vary from person to person based on how suggestible the individual with PTSD is. Sixty-seven PTSD participants agreed to take part in the research. Hypnotherapy, cognitive behavioral therapy, and counseling were the approaches used for these cases.

Research showed that people diagnosed with hypnotherapy as well as cognitive behavioral therapy, had fewer signs of PTSD six months after the session. Persons receiving advice alone had a higher level of lifestyle problems related to PTSD.

Those with hypnotherapy have reported lower re-experience incidences of the traumatic event.

People with PTSD will display up to 93% recovery after six hypnotherapy sessions.

The number is 72 percent with cognitive behavioral therapy after 22 sessions and 38 percent with psychotherapy after 600 sessions.

These research and figures show that hypnosis can be used to improve the quality of life of those with past trauma and unable to heal.

Individuals with PTSD are potentially more easily hypnotized than others. It raises the value of this treatment option for people suffering from post-traumatic stress disorders.

8 Tips for Understanding Someone with PTSD

PTSD makes it difficult to communicate. Most survivors cannot find words to describe what they feel. Even when they do, it's very natural for them not to share their experience comfortably. Elements of embarrassment, terror, anger, remorse, and sorrow sometimes impede a calm, concentrated debate.

Friends and families (and anyone else who is not the

PTSD trigger but stands by while someone is trying to cure) need a PTSD language translation. Through awareness, understanding, and empathy, you will have the best time to respond and connect during the healing process to your beloved PTSD. The more helpful and supportive you can be from the PTSD point of view. Now is the time for understanding, tolerance, and empathy.

#1. Power is information. Knowing the triggering mechanism, mental trauma reactions, PTSD warning signs, and symptoms, and the treatment options available to PTSD help you to understand better, maintain and direct your loved PTSD through diagnosis, care, and healing.

We need you to be straightforward, focused, and updated.

#2. Trauma affects us, trauma changes us. Upon trauma, we want to believe—as you do—that life will return like it was; that we can go on like what we were. It doesn't work like that. Trauma leaves a profound and indelible soul mark. Trauma cannot be felt, and a psychological transition cannot be witnessed.

Expect that we will be modified. Consider our evolutionary need. Join us on this trip. Help us.

#3. Our personality has been concealed by the PTSD. One of PTSD's biggest problems is that it takes over our whole view. We don't see clearly anymore. We don't see the world as we saw it before the trauma. It's dangerous, volatile, and challenging at every moment.

Remind us carefully and give us the opportunity to engage in an identity outside PTSD and trauma.

#4. We are not in our true self anymore. In the face of trauma, our true self-isolation and a healing self tend to shield us.

Believe in us, even if they are momentarily buried, our true selves still remain.

#5. How we act can't help us. We do not always monitor because we run on a kind of autopilot. PTSD is a survival mode exacerbated. We have feelings that make us nervous and overwhelmed. We behave in defense of those emotions that we are unable to control.

We often cannot avoid the frustration, tears, or other destructive habits that are so difficult for you to bear. Be patient with us.

#6. We can't make sense. Because our perspective is dominated by fear, we do not always think straight or follow the advice of those who do.

Even if your words don't seem to touch us, keep reaching out. You never know when we'll think of what you do, and it's going to ease, lead, relax, or encourage us.

#7. We can't 'get it' just. It's easy to imagine time from outside and memories fade away and pain is relegated to the past life. Unfortunately, nothing fades with PTSD. Our bodies are not going to let us forget. Due to the rising chemicals that enhance every memory, we can no longer walk away from the past than you can.

Honor our struggle with events to make peace. Do not hurry us. Do not pressure us. Trying to speed up our rehabilitation will only make us add more to it.

#8. We're not living in denial! Living with PTSD takes a tremendous effort. We know something is wrong, even if we don't admit it. When you approach us and deny that there is an issue that really codes for: "I do my best." To do what you say will need too much time, separate the emphasis from what holds us together. Sometimes just waking up and continuing our day-to-day routine is the first step in recovery. Reduce our tension by providing us with a safe place where we can find support.

CHAPTER 14

Can Medication Help?

Medicines have long been prescribed for the treatment of PTSD; drug treatment is not as effective as trauma-focused psychotherapies in persons with this disorder. I will put here the different medications used to treat PTSD and their effectiveness based on meta-analyses of randomized clinical trials. While medication is not considered a first-line treatment for PTSD, it may sometimes be necessary to relieve symptoms to the point that people are able and willing to engage in trauma-focused psychotherapies.

Case Vignette

Richard is a 25-year old married male serving in the U.S. Army and stationed in Afghanistan. This is his third deployment to the region, and while the first two deployments went well, the present one had been very difficult. Shortly after arriving in Kabul, his armored personnel carrier drove over an IED (improvised explosive device), killing a close buddy from his previous tours, riding with him and severely wounding another member of his team (leg severely crushed, likely needing amputation). Richard suffered a mild closed head injury from the blast but was alert enough after he awoke to realize the carnage around him. Shaken by this experience, he began experiencing frequent flashbacks of the explosion during the day and nightmares where he saw the faces and wounded bodies of his comrades. Unable to continue his duties over the next two months, he was evaluated by behavioral health, who diagnosed him with PTSD. As a result, Richard was sent back home to the U.S. to recover. Since this was his third and last deployment and he was ending the period of his enlistment, plans were made for his discharge from the military. His PTSD symptoms, however, persisted after returning home, affecting his ability to work and interfering with his family relationships. At his wife's encouragement, Richard scheduled an appointment at the local Veterans Affairs hospital for treatment. The psychologist who evaluated him at the VA confirmed the diagnosis of PTSD and recommended Prolonged Exposure Therapy (PET). After hearing about what this would entail, Richard refused. He could not imagine reliving the horrific experiences he had gone through in Afghanistan. The psychologist recommended he also see a psychiatrist, who after evaluating him, recommended a trial of paroxetine (trade name Paxil). Richard agreed and started the treatment. After four weeks, he noticed that his hyperarousal, anxiety and intrusive flashbacks were somewhat better, as was his sleep. The psychiatrist recommended he reconsider therapy with the psychologist. Now that he was feeling a bit better, Richard agreed and began a 3-month treatment program of weekly PET.

The reader is now warned. I will describe the medications used to treat PTSD and the research that has examined their effectiveness.

The various classes of medications used to treat PTSD (not all of which are recommended by current guidelines). These include antidepressants, anticonvulsants, antipsychotics, benzodiazepines, α1 adrenergic antagonists, glutaminergic agonists, and other somatic therapies

Antidepressants

The only medications for PTSD (and only if trauma-focused psychotherapies are not available or not preferred) currently recommended by the U.S. Food and Drug Administration are paroxetine and sertraline (i.e., serotonin reuptake inhibitors). These recommendations are now almost 10 years old (Stein et al., 2009). The American Psychological Association and Veterans Affairs/Department of Defense treatment guidelines have broadened the range of medications now recommended for PTSD to include paroxetine, sertraline, fluoxetine, and venlafaxine for the treatment of PTSD (and only these four medications).

Serotonin Reuptake Inhibitors (SSRIs). SSRIs inhibit the reuptake of serotonin in the space between neurons in the brain, making it more available for neuronal transmission. Defects in serotonin are thought to play an important part in the physiological abnormalities found in PTSD. In three meta-analyses involving more than 20 studies in over 3,000 patients, SSRI's overall have an ES ranging from -.23 to -.48, which indicates a small to moderate clinical effect (Watts et al., 2013; Hoskins et al., 2015; Lee et al., 2016). For individual SSRI's the ES of sertraline (Zoloft) ranges from -.13 to -.51 (again, small to moderate); for paroxetine (Paxil), the ES ranges from -.36 to -.74 (moderate); the ES of fluoxetine (Prozac) ranges from -.23 to -.43 (small to moderate); and for citalopram (Celexa), the range is +.13 to +.74 (this medication actually causes worse symptoms compared to placebo!). Note that SSRIs are the most commonly prescribed antidepressant for the treatment of Veterans with PTSD in Veterans Affairs (VA) hospitals and clinics (Bernardy et al., 2012). However, the ESs for SSRI's are dwarfed by those of trauma-focused psychotherapies that are typically -1.00 or larger, which is the basis for current recommendations.

Serotonin-Norepinephrine Reuptake Inhibitors (SNRIs). Of the two main SNRIs, venlafaxine (Effexor) and duloxetine (Cymbalta), only venlafaxine has been examined in a randomized clinical trial examining its efficacy in PTSD. Although there was an initial case report that PTSD symptom was made worse by duloxetine (Deneys & Ahearn, 2006), research since then has largely dispelled such concerns based on at least two 8-12-week open-label/naturalistic trials whose results were quite promising (Villareal et al., 2010; Walderhaug et al., 2010). With regard to venlafaxine, Watts et al (2013) and Hoskins et al (2015) reported small to moderate effect sizes

(-.20 to -.48) based on two large clinical trials. Although the FDA has not approved venlafaxine for the treatment of PTSD in the U.S., the British Association of Psychopharmacology considers venlafaxine to be a first-line medication (Baldwin et al., 2014). Venlafaxine is also one of the four antidepressants recommended by the VA/DoD (2017) and APA (2017) practice guidelines as monotherapy for PTSD in patients who choose not to engage in or are unable to access trauma-focused psychotherapy.

Other Newer Antidepressants. A number of newer antidepressants, relative to older drugs (tricyclic antidepressants and monoamine oxidase inhibitors), have been examined for their benefits in treating PTSD. These include mirtazapine, bupropion, and nefazodone. Mirtazapine (Remeron), a serotonin and norepinephrine reuptake inhibitor with antihistaminic effects, is a relatively safe antidepressant that is sedating and increases appetite in those with weight loss. Watts et al. (2013) and Lee et al. (2016) reported that a single study of 29 patients (Davidson et al., 2003) found that mirtazapine's effects on PTSD symptoms did not differ from placebo over an 8-week trial on most PTSD measures. Bupropion (Wellbutrin), a norepinephrine and dopamine reuptake inhibitor (two catecholamines involved in emotional disorders), tends to increase energy, improve concentration, and reduce appetite, and like mirtazapine, is a relatively safe drug for use in middle-aged and older adults with other medical problems. Based on a single trial of 22 patients (Becker et al., 2007), both Watts et al and Lee et al reported that the effect of bupropion on PTSD symptoms assessed by the Clinician Assessed PTSD Scale (CAPS; the standard measure of PTSD symptoms in clinical trials today) did not differ from placebo in the 8-week trial. Finally, nefazodone (Serzone)—a moderate reuptake inhibitor of both serotonin and norepinephrine—is a sedating antidepressant (although less sedating than trazodone [Desyrel], its cousin). Based on a single study of 41 patients (Davis et al., 2004), nefazodone reduced PTSD symptoms on CAPS during a 12-week trial compared to placebo with a moderate ES (-.60) that achieved statistical significance ($p=0.04$). However, clinicians seldom use nefazodone today due to reports of liver toxicity.

Tricyclic Antidepressants (TCAs). TCAs such as amitriptyline, imipramine, nortriptyline, and desipramine are an older class of antidepressants that have lots of side-effects, including weight gain, sedation, anticholinergic, and cardiovascular effects. They are seldom used today now that SSRIs, NSRIs, and other safer antidepressants are available. Watts et al. (2013), one of the few meta-analyses of TCA effectiveness in PTSD, indicated a small effect (ES=-0.36, not different from placebo) based on three studies involving 110 patients.

Monoamine Oxidase Inhibitors (MAOIs). MAOIs such as phenelzine, tranylcypromine, and brofaromine are another class of older antidepressants that block the degradation of monoamine neurotransmitters (norepinephrine, serotonin, etc.), and like TCAs, are very effective for treating depression but have a host of unpleasant side-effects (weight gain, hypotension, and hypertensive crisis unless careful with diet to avoid tyramine-containing foods/drinks). Interestingly, in the first randomized clinical trial to examine the effectiveness of medication for the treatment of PTSD in 1988, an MAOI (phenelzine) and a TCA (imipramine) were compared to placebo in 34 combat Veterans with PTSD. They found that the MAOI (compared to the TCA) was particularly more effective than a placebo (Frank et al., 1988). However, Hoskins et al (2015) and Lee et al (2016), who reported on the results from two clinical trials involving the MAOI brofaromine (Consonar), did not find a difference compared to placebo when treating PTSD.

Antidepressants Overall. Watts et al (2013) reported that the overall effect of antidepressants on reducing PTSD symptoms compared to placebo in 32 randomized controlled trials involving 4,276 patients was small to moderate (ES=-.43, 95% CI=-.31 to -.53), justifying their use in the treatment of PTSD (but again as a second-line treatment after psychotherapy). Nearly three-quarters (70%) of patients with PTSD seen at VA hospitals and clinics are now prescribed an antidepressant (NPEC, 2016).

Anticonvulsants

There is uniform agreement among all the meta-analyses that anticonvulsants (i.e., anti-seizures drugs that are often used as mood stabilizers in bipolar disorder, including divalproex [Depakote], topiramate, and tiagabine, etc.) have no role in the treatment of PTSD. In none of these did the effects of anticonvulsants when used along with or combined with antidepressants exceed the effects of placebo in reducing PTSD symptoms. Watts et al. (2013) reported a meta-analysis of results from 7 studies of anticonvulsants involving 388 patients and found no significant effects compared to placebo; the same conclusion was reached by a more recent review by Lee et al (2016). There is some evidence that lamotrigine (Lamictal; an anticonvulsant used in bipolar disorder specifically for bipolar depression) has been useful in treating PTSD, although the evidence is not strong and does not justify recommending it.

Antipsychotics

Antipsychotics (used to treat psychotic symptoms), even newer second-generation drugs such as risperidone (Risperdal), olanzapine (Zyprexa), quetiapine (Seroquel), and aripiprazole (Abilify), play little role in the treatment of PTSD and none of the consensus guidelines recommend them, despite their small to moderate effects that differ significantly from placebo (ESs ranging from -.39 to -.49) (Watts et al., 2013; Lee et al., 2016). The main reason for not recommending these drugs is their side effects. Those effects include significant weight gain, increased blood sugar (especially in diabetics), risk of cardiovascular effects in older adults (including heart attack, death, and stroke), and extrapyramidal symptoms. Extrapyramidal symptoms are Parkinson-like symptoms (shaking, muscle stiffness, slowed movements) that were common in first-generation antipsychotics like haloperidol (Haldol) or chlorpromazine (Thorazine), even though they are less common with second-generation antipsychotics. Combining antipsychotics with antidepressants does not help either, where benefits of doing so have been no greater than placebo.

CHAPTER 15

PSTD Methods

Individuals with post-traumatic stress disorder (PTSD) regularly battle with visits and exceptional manifestations of nervousness. These solid side effects of nervousness frequently lead individuals with PTSD to depend on undesirable methods for adapting, for example, through medication or liquor use. Luckily, there are various solid methods for adapting to nervousness that may enable your uneasiness to go down in power, become less regular, and additionally become increasingly decent.

Profound Breathing

Profound breathing can be a significant adapting expertise to learn. It might sound senseless, however, numerous individuals don't inhale appropriately.

Regular breathing includes your stomach, an enormous muscle in your belly. At the point when you take in, your gut ought to grow. At the point when you inhale out, your midsection should fall. After some time, individuals overlook how to inhale along these lines and rather utilize their chest and shoulders. This causes short and shallow breaths, which can build pressure and nervousness. Luckily, it isn't past the point where it is possible to "re-realize" how to inhale and help shield yourself from stress. Practice this straightforward exercise to improve your breathing and battle uneasiness.

Dynamic Muscle Relaxation

Utilizing unwinding activities can be a successful method to lessen your pressure and tension. One unwinding activity called dynamic muscle unwinding centers around an individual switching back and forth among straining and loosening up various muscle bunches all through the body. This unwinding strategy is like a pendulum. The complete unwinding of your muscles can be gotten by first setting off to the next outrageous (that is, by straining your muscles). Likewise, by straining your muscles (a typical manifestation of uneasiness) and quickly loosening up them, the side effect of muscle pressure may turn into a sign to unwind after some time. You can gain proficiency with a fundamental dynamic muscle unwinding exercise in this article.

Care

Utilizing care for uneasiness can be useful. Care has been around for a very long time. Nonetheless, psychological wellness experts are starting to perceive that care can have numerous advantages for individuals experiencing challenges, for example, nervousness and despondency. Basically, care is tied in with being in contact with and mindful of the present minute. So frequently in our lives, we are latched onto our subconscious minds, made up for lost time in the uneasiness and stresses of everyday life. This activity will acquaint you with care and might be useful for getting you "out of your head" and in contact with the present minute.

Self-Monitoring

Self-observing can be a useful method for understanding your tension indications. We are all "animals of propensity." We regularly approach our day without deduction, being uninformed of much that goes on around us. This might be helpful in certain circumstances, however different occasions, this absence of mindfulness may make us feel as if our considerations and feelings are totally capricious and unmanageable. We can't generally address awkward side effects of uneasiness without first monitoring what circumstances raise these sentiments. Self-observing is a basic method for expanding this mindfulness.

Social Support

Again, and again, it has been discovered that discovering support from others can be a central point in helping individuals defeat the negative impacts of a horrible mishap and PTSD. Having somebody, you believe that you can converse with can be exceptionally useful for working through upsetting circumstances or for passionate approval. Be that as it may, basically having somebody accessible to converse with may not be sufficient. There are a few significant pieces to a steady relationship that might be especially valuable in helping somebody deal with their nervousness.

Self-Soothing

At the point when you are encountering tension, it is imperative to have methods for adapting to those emotions. For instance, searching out social help can be an astounding method for improving your state of mind. Be that as it may, the uneasiness related to side effects of PTSD can here and there happen surprisingly, and social help may not be promptly accessible. In this manner, it is critical to pick up adapting procedures that you can do without anyone else. Adapting techniques concentrated on improving your mindset and decreasing the tension that you can do individually are now and again depicted as self-calming or self-care adapting procedures.

Expressive Writing

Utilizing journaling to adapt to and express your contemplations and sentiments (additionally called expressive composition) can be a decent method for adapting to tension. Expressive composing has been found to improve physical and mental wellbeing. As to PTSD specifically, expressive composing has been found to have various advantages, including improved adapting and posttraumatic development (or the capacity to discover importance in and have positive life changes following an awful mishap), just as decreased PTSD side effects, pressure, and outrage.

Interruption

Deliberate utilization of interruption strategies can really be of advantage in adapting to feelings that are solid and feel awkward, for example, tension and dread. Interruption is anything you do to briefly remove your consideration from forceful feeling. Some of the time, concentrating on a forceful feeling can make it feel significantly more grounded and progressively crazy. Subsequently, by incidentally diverting yourself, you may give the feeling some an opportunity to diminish in force, making it simpler to oversee.

Conduct Activation

Uneasiness and shirking go connected at the hip. While the shirking of uneasiness inciting circumstances may help diminish our tension right now, in the long haul, it might keep us from carrying on with an important and compensating life (particularly as this evasion becomes greater and greater). Conduct initiation is an extraordinary method for expanding your action level, just as the amount you take part in positive and remunerating exercises. Through social actuation, you can lessen your downturn and tension.

CHAPTER 16

About PTSD & Triggers

Figuring out what sets a PTSD partner off takes work and knowledge. When you have unmanaged PTSD, almost anything prompts negative feelings and emotions. A trigger can be any situation, person, place, smell, noise, or object that elicits uncomfortable and unwelcome emotional and physical symptoms. Triggers act as the catalyst for flashbacks (reliving memories) and can negatively influence behavior and affect how the person perceives their surrounding environment.

While some triggers are obvious, others are more difficult to recognize and tackle. A military veteran might be triggered by loud sounds like gunfire, so avoiding these situations will reduce the chances of the person being triggered. A child abuse and neglect survivor might be triggered by a smell in an elevator and not immediately identify or understand the cause.

PTSD triggers can be internal or external in nature. Internal triggers are things the person experiences inside their own body and mind. These can include thoughts, memories, emotions, physical sensations, and the like. External triggers are any outside influences the person encounters throughout the day. Situations, places, people, or other things that happen outside the body are external triggers.

Identifying PTSD Triggers

It may feel as if PTSD symptoms occur spontaneously, but this is not the case. PTSD symptoms generally occur after a trigger sets them off. The best way to prevent "out of control" situations is to learn about and pinpoint triggers, and you can do this as a couple. You must learn to become aware of them and manage them ahead of time before they disrupt the day.

To counteract the unnecessary reactivity that triggers have on the PTSD brain, the PTSD partner must learn ways to identify occurrences, situations, and behaviors that tend to trigger symptoms. Anyone can learn to anticipate these triggers, distance from them, or get in front of them and take appropriate action to prevent them from having an impact on your life and romantic relationship. Be aware that increasing awareness of triggers can bring distress, but it's important to fight through and conquer the fear to move forward.

By nature, traumatic experiences are distressing, and post-traumatic reactions of shock and distress are normal. Most people recover naturally, helped by adequate social support.

Common External Triggers

- Trauma reminders and arguments
- Witnessing a car accident
- Certain sounds, sights, or smells
- A relationship ending
- Family, school, work, money, or relationships
- Specific dates
- Holidays
- A specific place
- A personal reminder of trauma
- Nature (weather, seasons, etc.)
- Hospitals, medical treatment, funerals

Common Internal Triggers

- Anxiety
- Anger
- Sadness

- Strong emotions (helplessness, trapped)
- Bad memories
- Frustration
- Feeling lonely
- Feeling out of control
- Feeling vulnerable
- Increased heartbeat
- Muscle tension pain

Coping with PTSD Triggers

The most effective way of coping with triggers is to avoid them, but this is nearly impossible to do because emotions, thoughts, and physical sensations cannot really be avoided. When a person with PTSD is struggling with self-regulation, their thoughts, emotions, and sensations are all over the place. While you can take steps to manage exposure to external triggers, internal triggers are more difficult to manage. Either way, without effective coping strategies, managing any triggers can be a frightening task with the potential to negatively impact the relationship. Here are some examples of coping approaches. All of them can be practiced as a couple's activity because techniques and strategies to cope with PTSD symptoms can serve to reduce anxiety and benefit both PTSD and non-PTSD people:

- Mindfulness
- Calm (Diaphragmatic) Breathing
- Progressive Muscle Relaxation
- Self-Soothing Techniques
- Grounding
- Expressive Writing (Journaling)
- Grounding
- Visualization

A variety of coping strategies will make trigger management much easier. Healthy coping strategies can also help to retrain the PTSD brain after trauma, making the PTSD partner more likely to prevent the development of unhealthy or faulty coping mechanisms. Before practicing any techniques to identify and manage triggers, be sure you have a safety plan in place, just in case, things get too distressing.

Living with a PTSD Partner

As the life-impacting disorder that it is, PTSD can take a heavy toll on relationships. The symptoms that accompany the disorder can make it difficult for the sufferer to accommodate the intricacies of a relationship, and for the non-PTSD partner to understand the behavior of their loved one with PTSD. PTSD has a profound effect on a person's ability to provide affection and makes them more volatile. A non-PTSD partner who is not prepared or knowledgeable may feel as if they are constantly walking on eggshells or living with a stranger.

It is difficult for a non-PTSD partner not to take the accompanying symptoms of PTSD personally. It's imperative to understand that a person with PTSD is not always in control of their actions and reactions. Often, they are trapped in an uncomfortable and difficult to navigate constant state of alert that increases their feelings of vulnerability, fear, shame, guilt, and makes them feel unsafe all the time. PTSD symptoms cannot be turned off, so here are a few pointers to consider when living with a partner who has PTSD.

Remaster the Art of Listening

While people with PTSD should not be pressured into talking about their traumatic experience, they will talk when they are ready. If they choose to share their experience, it is important for a non-PTSD partner to **be a good listener** without being judgmental. Sometimes the act of listening is more valuable than any advice. Listening without expectations shows that you are interested and that you care what the other person has to say, not that you care; they listen to what you have to say.

A good, knowledgeable, and caring non-PTSD partner can be the catalyst for change in the life of their partner. If your PTSD partner feels comfortable enough to talk, because you're a good and attentive listener, they might want to **talk about the traumatic event repeatedly.** There is nothing wrong with it, and this is part of their healing process. The non-PTSD partner should avoid telling their partner to stop revisiting the past and move on, even if the details are difficult to listen to. Respect their feelings if you want them to trust you and open to you for healing.

Provide Social Support

Often, non-PTSD partners lack a basic understanding of what life is like for a person with PTSD. The impact and far-reaching effects of the accompanying symptoms can make a person be in a constant state of anger, irritability, depression, mistrust, guilt, shame, and many other negative feelings and emotions.

A solid, loving, and caring **support system** can help the PTSD partner move away from the traumatic experience, instead of living in a constant state of anxiety that makes them want to withdraw from friends and family.

It might not always be easy to demonstrate love, support, and affection to someone suffering from PTSD, but simply being there for them can play a major role in their healing journey and process.

Don't pressure your PTSD loved one into talking about their trauma or what they might be feeling now. It can be extremely difficult for a person with PTSD to share details about their traumatic experiences and could worsen things. Be there for them when they are ready to talk or simply 'hang out' when they don't feel like a chatterbox.

Be patient with your PTSD partner. Recovery from PTSD is a long and tedious process that may involve setbacks. Don't be judgmental, be accepting, and patient about your partner's progress (or regress).

Especially during stressful times, try your best to **engage in normal activities**, those that have nothing to do with PTSD, or serve as a reminder of the trauma. It could be doing a hobby you both enjoy dancing, going for a walk, watching a movie, or hundreds of other options.

Help Rebuild Trust & Safety

PTSD fundamentally alters the way people view the world because the traumatic experience leaves the person feeling unsafe, on edge, fragile, and feeling as if, at any given moment, the trauma will repeat. These negative feelings take a toll on a person's sense of trust and safety and can become serious hurdles in romantic relationships.

As a non-PTSD partner, part of your job is to **help rebuild** your PTSD partner's surrounding world from a constantly dangerous and frightening place to a safe and trustworthy one that helps reduce anxiety. A good way to help rebuild trust and safety is to **create a solid and predictable routine** you can both follow. A structured and foreseeable world tends to reduce anxiety in people with PTSD and can help restore the lost sense of stability, security, and safety stolen by PTSD symptoms. From grocery shopping to house cleaning, to cooking, to mealtimes, anything that provides structure and organization will serve to reduce the constant feelings of lack of safety and trust.

By helping your PTSD partner rebuild, you are contributing to their ability to trust themselves and others again, a crucial component of PTSD recovery. Helping a person with PTSD rebuild trust and safety takes **work and commitment**, so make sure your partner knows you're in for the long-haul.

CHAPTER 17

Recovery and Daily Home life Demands

Life's Normal Demands

Typically, after short or long durations of emergencies or traumatic events, individuals become disorganized in daily life tasks. Clothes are unwashed and unfolded. Trash stacks up. Dishes are unclean. Cars are filthy. Bed sheets unchanged. Bills unpaid. The grass didn't mow. Children neglected. Friendships ignored. Spouses unheeded. All daily chores or everyday relationships are pushed to the side when urgent events must take priority. Overtime work, double/triple shifts, and exhausting schedules sidetrack normal living necessities. Physical fatigue, emotional exhaustion, and mental flooding leave nothing left for daily, ordinary demands.

When recovering from the demands of trauma work,

we find ourselves now overwhelmed with unsolved problems at home, unfinished tasks, irritating chores, desk clutter. We have odd conflicts with loved ones who need loving attention. You are exhausted, yet ordinary demands piled-up in your absence. In order to recover from your trauma work, you will need to rest and recalibrate your body's physical needs. Next, you will need to practice simple restorative inner peace exercises that help you regain mental and emotional space for recovery. Then, you will need to pay attention to the chores of daily life that you have left unattended.

We will walk you through step-by-step ways of resolving these "nagging" chores. Pick-up the pieces of your "normal" life. Reorganize daily life that has become chaotic. Fortunately, resolving daily ordinary problems will help you 1) clear up the emotional clutter of normal life messes, 2) re-integrate you back into your daily home life and identity, and 3) repair damage created by neglect, exhaustion, and distractions associated with your work with trauma.

First Steps

Five steps below will help you deal with your home life demands:

1. Be patient with yourself.
2. Take each day and each day's tasks, one step at a time.
3. Use the procrastination tools that motivate you or help you regain your daily functions.
4. Clearly, communicate with your family and friends about your level of stress, fatigue, or exhaustion. This will help them comprehend what steps you are taking to recover and why you need to pace yourself.
5. Communicate with your family and friends your plans for recovery. Tell them your plans so they can a) help you recover, b) be patient with you, c) anticipate that their lives too will return to normalcy.

Second Steps

Now, we will give you four tools to motivate your otherwise demotivated energies to get some chores done. Daily tasks may look too big, too foreboding, or too boring. After all, work-life is horribly demanding, and the last thing you want to do is more work at home. You want home life to be a refuge. Yet, home life has chores too. The family has desires and needs too.

Frustrating isn't it, especially when you are recovering from trauma work. We will begin with the "Just-Get-It-Done" approach.

Mental Attitude Trick #1: The "Just-Get-IT-Done" Mantra

"Just-Get-IT-Done" can become your mental declaration that leads you to finish those tasks, which are staring you in the face.

"Just-Get-IT-Done" can become a mantra. Mantras are meaningful words or phrases we repeat throughout our day, which aim to steer our attitudes, emotions, and actions.

"Just-Get-IT-Done NOW!" becomes an answer to yourself any time you feel inclined to:

   a. Procrastinate
   b. Delay
   c. Avoid
   d. Pass-it-on to someone else to do

"Just-Get-IT-Done" becomes the coach on your shoulder shouting in your ears to ACT NOW.

Typically, after you begin your task, having coerced yourself with **"Just-Get-IT-Done"**, you feel less burdened, you feel more productive and organized, and you also enjoy hanging out with your new proactive self.

So, this "**Just-Get-IT-Done**" mantra is one of many tools you can use to help you resolve or finish whatever is stopping you.

Mental Attitude Trick #2: "Get Your Ass in Gear, Dude"

Some individuals wisely hassle themselves or "yell-at" themselves when they need to tackle something. Wisely hassle themselves? Yes. Sometimes. We occasionally have to become irritated with ourselves enough to kick us into action. Irritation can motivate us to finish washing dishes, pay bills, make appointments, or complete daunting projects. We wisely can use our agitated or angry feelings to motivate us when we are stalled, avoiding something, or feeling confused or indecisive.

Those people who function best "in the last-minute," use stress to wake up their brains and focus their efforts and time. Yes, procrastinators wake-up under pressure too. People with ADHD diagnoses often do their last-minute accomplishments in a harried state. When they are rushed, a task gets done. Then, they flow back to their "chill zone."

We respond quickly when we are in a crisis. Trauma work can train your body and mind to only respond when there is an emergency and be passive when nothing is urgent. This can make ordinary home life chores harder to do because they may not seem urgent. "Get Your Ass in Gear, Dude" is a mental way of tricking your brain and body into action even when there is no emergency.

So, as you reintegrate back into your normal daily home routines, every so often, you might decide to pressure yourself with a little self-kicking such as "Get Your Ass in Gear, Dude." Chances are you will feel better after you have gotten something done that was nagging at you.

Depression and Anxiety Due to Unresolved Daily Tasks

Individuals ask me to help them stop being panicked or anxious after a traumatic event. Interestingly, one of the dimensions of their panic or anxiety can be related to unresolved aspects of their ordinary lives. A normal unresolved issue is harassing them, making them feel very demotivated, agitated, irritable, or upset. After they resolve those daily issues, a sweet calmness often settles into place. They feel internal conflicts and tensions gently soothing because they have solved the daily issues or finished the normal tasks hanging over their heads. For them, their agitation was a signal that something in their everyday life needed to get done.

Face it though, we all have unfinished projects or chores, all the time. If we live perpetually in a state of anxiety because something is not done, we will spiral into the cortisol-slaved-stress that kidnaps our body's health, our brain's clarity, and our inner peace.

Clearly, even after trauma work, we have to finish what we can in our home life. Yet, we must be patient with our progress and energy levels. Practice our Inner Peace tools. Motivate ourselves to face dreaded chores. Grow our ability to function efficiently in our normal life, one step at a time.

CHAPTER 18

To Family and Friends

It is so very important to know and understand that your loved one is sick, lonely, unable-to-change, guilt-ridden, and shame-filled. If they could do better, they would do better. They need treatment. Good, focused professional care is required for these afflictions. Your first job is this knowledge. You also must love them in a clear, demonstrative way. And it is very important that you insist that their treatment be focused on "The Big Five" values of recovery. It is also very important that you participate in their treatment and offer consistent, ongoing support in their recovery efforts.

This stuff is not easy. You will be challenged to detach emotionally, work on yourself, and stay the course in clarity and love. Your own support system is essential. Support groups such as Al-Anon are so very helpful in this regard. They have much to offer around acceptance, understanding, and specific methods for coping and thriving in these situations. Work your own program of recovery. Getting therapy, having your own personal spiritual practice of prayer, meditation, inspirational reading, and time spent in nature are all helpful in this regard. If in Al-Anon, or another 12 Step group, actually working those steps can be a tremendous asset for your personal growth and well-being. The rewards are tremendous. To witness the benefits of long-term, full recovery from any or all of these afflictions is a great, uplifting life experience. It is happening every day, everywhere, and it can happen in the life of your loved one. Stay the course. The miracle of recovery is something not to be missed. You can allow for this to take place in your life. It is truly worth every minute spent doing the work. May you embark on this path and reap all the joy.

To Treatment Providers

I feel such a deep sense of connection to you, my brothers and sisters working in this noble profession. I know full well the challenges you face day in and day out around these difficult to treat afflictions. These work environments are so highly charged with negative emotions and human suffering, that just holding up to the barrage of it all is enough to cause doubt about your choice of careers. Yet, the upside of great reward in terms of witnessing a complete transformation in the recovery process is something that keeps you in the game, coming back each day for more.

I commend you and honor you for doing God's work. This effort is nothing short of life-saving and clearly quality-of-life enhancing. Give yourself credit for your efforts and knowledge. Know that you make a difference. Embrace the process and release the outcomes. Support your fellow team members and love the afflicted ones. Keep on keeping on, never giving in to discouragement or loss of hope for anyone. Be an enthusiastic advocate for recovery each day. Grow yourself. Know that the problem is brain-based/physical/psychological, and the solution is spiritual. Do not take anything personally while always doing your best each day. Believe!

Have clarity and focus. I remember when seeing an orthopedic specialist following a leg injury, I was told that RICE would be the best treatment. So, Rest, Ice, Compression, and Elevation is what worked. All working in that field agreed on this path. They all were on the same page.

Can we do the same? Sobriety/Stability/Safety, Love, Unity, Growth, and Spirituality (SLUGS) is the best treatment for addiction, mental illness, and PTSD. Let's get on the same page.

Note: I have addressed three afflictions together due to their common co-occurrence. It is essential that when we see any one of these, we also look for the presence of a second or third diagnosis. So many who are addicted also suffer from PTSD and/or mental illness. There is a great amount of commonality and cross-over with these disorders. Treatment can and should be designed for this consideration.

For Prevention

Prevention efforts need to focus on the truth. These afflictions are truly illnesses of the brain, a part of the body. No judgment allowed. The truth around which drugs are most addictive, who is more susceptible to these afflictions, and the real-life impact that occurs are topics worthy of focused discussion. Family-of-origin, heredity, and trauma all need attention. Adverse childhood experiences (ACE) need to be included as considerations for causation and those impacted need to be identified as high risk and helped accordingly. Most young people will not be fooled by some of the messages we have provided in the past. Be honest. For example, the truth about opiate drugs is that they are highly addictive, much more so than many of the others. The message should be "it is so good, don't even try it once." Give information about the vast and rising numbers of overdose deaths. Tell the truth about how some illegal, "street" drugs like marijuana and magic mushrooms are not so addictive, nor do they have much mortality associated, and have shown to benefit certain medical/psychiatric/addiction type conditions.

In Summary

We have to do better. The death rate for these afflictions has been on a steady increase for years. Knowledge and action must have clarity and focus. We need a firm foundation for our field and our efforts around caring for those with these afflictions. We need to know, understand, accept, embrace, and love the addicted, the mentally ill, and the traumatized in order to provide the highest level of care.

If you have one or more of these afflictions, get quality professional care, insisting on focused treatment that emphasizes complete recovery. Believe that you can experience total healing and gain long-term recovery. Life can become amazingly fulfilling and so beautiful. You can and will ascend to your highest functioning, realizing your life potential and purpose. Peace of mind is a goal that we all share. Recovery will deliver. Go for it. It is so worth it.

CHAPTER 19

Curing PTSD with EFT, Meditation, and Energy

Emotional trauma release is an intense release of a certain emotion that has been stored either in the body or the mind due to a traumatic event or repressed feelings that have accumulated over time. The emotion can be released directly through physical activity or physical therapies (such as massage) or it can be triggered by your environment or through reactions to things that others say or do. When emotions surface, you can be overwhelmed with anger, fear, sadness, hopelessness, or any other emotion, often without explanation of why you feel this way. I would experience this intense release of emotion during meditation and EFT sessions as well as from other triggers during everyday interaction and massage therapy.

Physical trauma release occurs when you release a memory of a painful experience that has been stored within a specific area in your body. The memory is released through a sequence of physical symptoms similar to the pain you experienced at the time of the trauma. The pain varies in intensity from person to person and maybe a revisit of symptoms you felt during the initial experience or a mild form of those symptoms. I would sometimes experience a few minutes of physical symptoms that were so intense it would leave me feeling disoriented for a while afterward. Sometimes it would follow with an emotional release. It would always come with a slight warning so that I could get into a safe environment before the symptoms started. I always felt so much better for the release immediately afterward, feeling a sense of less tension and more peace and present awareness. However, I was not prepared for the longest trauma release I've ever had.

During the last year, I briefly encountered an episode of post-traumatic stress. It was not a present traumatic event that set it off, but a past traumatic event that was triggered through a dream. I had no memory of it and still don't. It lasted 3 weeks, but it felt like an eternity. I had intense anxiety, constant nausea and chest pain, thoughts that seemed to stimulate my worst fears and anxieties, nightmares, night sweats, heart palpitations, a lot of physical pain during the day, and worse during the night.

Around the time before and during those weeks, I seemed to meet a lot of clients suffering from similar symptoms of PTSD that did not understand what was going on or how to get it under control. They were suffering from it for months. That scared me. I wasn't sure how I'd cope if this continued for that long! Luckily using my professional knowledge of self-healing techniques, I was able to use a combination of EFT and meditation techniques to get the symptoms under control and have periods of time (at least a few hours per day) where I had no symptoms at all and felt relatively normal). I can't say how long I would have suffered with it if I didn't have meditation tools and EFT to get through it as fast as I did. Having had this experience and trialed the same techniques on clients with PTSD I feel passionate about sharing the techniques with you so that you or someone close to you with PTSD can experience a faster road to recovery.

The combination of techniques I used included EFT (Emotional Freedom Technique, commonly known as Tapping), energy healing and meditation, and making sure I kept myself engaged in positive activities that I was passionate about as this kept my natural endorphin level at its highest. By doing this, it kept me in a positive frame of mind, which encouraged me to focus on improving my quality of life rather than focusing on the negative experience I was going through.

After reading this e-book, using the techniques described above, you will be able to:

Use EFT in 3 different ways: firstly, to reduce intense PTSD symptoms, then to manage and control your symptoms, and lastly, to fully heal from PTSD using Meditative EFT (combining meditation and EFT).

Use a short bedtime ritual to ensure that sleep is more of a sound and peaceful nature; nightmares are kept to a minimum and it becomes a productive sleep, not a traumatic one. Also, use it to go back to sleep during the night and settle yourself and your body in the morning after a difficult night to start the day feeling the best you can.

Learn the basics of meditation and use it to get better results with EFT so that you don't have to wait until your symptoms are critical before you work further on your PTSD, maintaining a better sense of control over symptoms and enabling you to take control of your own healing.

Learn the basics of energy healing through meditation. Use it on yourself to lift your mood after an EFT session enabling you to continue with your day feeling positive and uplifted.

Understand how to find your passions in life and becoming involved with them can activate your endorphins, which are your most powerful healer and steer your life into a more positive direction.

CHAPTER 20

Trauma Treatment and Mental Health

Trauma treatment might be a rather new term to some, but too many common. Cognitive-behavioral therapy is a type of mental therapy that helps or enables one to deal with their thoughts and balance their daily mental state. This involves one's surrounding in terms of their societal constraints as well as actions and how they affect them in one way or another or their feelings. This is a study that will help you keep a profile of some of the things that trigger you emotionally as well as how to manage and contain them. Just as the name entails, it is therapy done to treat mental conditions that are caused by past experiences or situations that impacted one's wellbeing. That is conditions or ailments such as depressions or even anxiety. Yes, depression is an ailment. As we all know that when someone is depressed beyond measures, they can handle, they are prone to self-destruct or self-inflict injuries or mostly commonly abuse drugs. Trauma Treatment is not only for mental but also physical wellness as well.

This has always been a study under review and many have benefited from it in society. Its zeros in majorly on the challenges in the society or community at large that are not necessarily treatable through medicating or normal hospital appointments. Many have mental or behavioral distortions unknowingly, but when addressed and carefully decrypted, you'll find that there's always one thing that can do trigger a person not to be or act themselves. Trauma treatment help improves and uplifts one's personal emotional as well as social or even physical regulation by providing lasting and long-term solutions and strategies that add up to solving and diagnosing conditions.

The main aim of trauma treatment is to help an individual with previous problems, boost happiness as well as get rid of sadness and upgrade and treat dysfunctional and wrecked emotions one may harbor in them. As we all know, emotions affect our every move as well as influence them in one way or another. That is our behaviors, actions as well as thoughts. Trauma treatment is mainly rooted in providing and implementing effective solutions that will help an individual outgrow previous toxic habits and traits as well as uplift and encourage them to change destructive norms they take value in as well as uphold.

CONCLUSION

While it's up to you to do the hard work, a critical part of your success depends on the strength of support you have from the people around you. Whether you already have some of these supportive relationships or are working to develop them in the future, relying on them will help get you through the rough spots. It doesn't matter if support comes from your partner, friends, family members, clergy, coworkers, classmates, or neighbors. Just work on building a strong, supportive network of people you can count on and who can count on you in return.

It can be comforting to connect with other trauma survivors or people with similar recovery goals. The more you tell others about your experience, goals, and type of support you want, the more you'll find secure and stable sources of support.

If you've isolated yourself or used avoidance extensively, your current network may be limited. This may also be true if you've been depressed or angry and have pushed others away. Regardless, part of getting active for you will include increasing your personal contacts. It's okay to start small. Say hello to a neighbor or coworker or reach out to someone in an online forum. In-person or online support groups can also provide support when you need it most.

Take notice of the people currently in your life who already offer steady support. PTSD can be difficult to understand, even when you're the one suffering from it. Not everyone will be a good source of support. Others around you will have their own reactions to your traumatic experience or have their own personal struggles to deal with that make it difficult for them to offer the kind of help you need. Support from a loved one may come in the form of a comforting hand during Fourth of July fireworks, time spent together after a difficult day, a friend accompanying you to the doctor, or a knowing look when you seem at the end of a short fuse.

Appreciate the people who are supportive and find compassion for them when they fall short or have their own difficulties. Supporting someone with PTSD is challenging, and your loved ones are probably suffering in response to your pain and suffering. Keep in mind that there will be times that the support you need may not come in the package you expect. Support may be your 12-Step sponsor insisting you attend a meeting, or your spouse telling you to get out of bed and drive your child to school. Think about why they're asking you to do something uncomfortable and recognize that it may be the exact encouragement you need.

Asking for, and sometimes even accepting, support requires vulnerability. If someone were physically injured, you'd need to know where it hurt before you could provide first aid. PTSD is tough because there's no physical mark. You may look okay on the outside even though you're struggling. This is very confusing for everyone around you. It doesn't mean that others can't or won't rise to the occasion and offer what you need, but ultimately, it's not their job to take charge of your recovery—it's yours. Even if your trauma occurred through no fault of your own or in the service of others, your symptoms and your recovery are your responsibility.

www.ingramcontent.com/pod-product-compliance
Lightning Source LLC
Chambersburg PA
CBHW071619080526
44588CB00010B/1197